D1157594

# The
# Digital
# Mindset

How to Retool Your Skills and
Rewire Your Brain
for the Digital Age

## Carol Ingley

Media Mogul Series

**Media Mogul Press**
Washington, D.C.

Media Mogul Press is a division of Be a Media Mogul.

For information about special discounts for bulk sales of *The Digital Mindset*, please contact Media Mogul Press at www.MediaMogulPress.com.

*The Digital Mindset* is second in the *Media Mogul Series* of books.

*The Digital Mindset* contains the opinions, views and market forecasts of the author.

Manufactured in the United States of America

ISBN 978-0-9797174-2-0

Library of Congress Control Number: 2011902750

# The
# Digital
# Mindset

*To Herbert A. and
Mary Borum Ingley*

*and to*

*Fletcher and
Dorothy Callis Martin*

*all my love and thanks*

**Be the change you wish

to see in the world.**

**—Mahatma Gandhi**

# Contents

# Preface

*The Digital Mindset* is about how to retool for the digital age. The telecommunications, information technology, and Internet industries have already gone through the retooling process. It is time for the U.S. citizen and citizens of the world to retool as well. This book is also about shifting from status quo thinking to digital thinking.

In October 2002, I inadvertently discovered the digital mindset. It came out of several years of research for a market study that I authored and published on global broadband. The study looked at PCs, TVs, broadband Internet, cable TV service, satellite TV service, voice service, and any number of other services and technologies in all households of the major countries around the globe. It was a comprehensive 500-page report.

Then, there was a single moment when I stopped in my tracks. In the flash of a second, it became very clear that, once content was all digital and once devices were all digital, anything was possible. What was not possible was to envision a marketplace using the business forecasting tools that had worked so well for my business in the past. How do you forecast a marketplace with so many possibilities? I stopped selling the study and it became my business plan.

The world as I began to see it was heading toward something so different that, once observed, there was no going back. I could not "undo" the new mindset into which I had stumbled. As I have enjoyed over time that "undo" function in Microsoft Office, I almost wished in 2002 that I could have pushed that sort of key, for the outlook was ahead of the technology and ahead of the time. I was in a strange sort of limbo that, thankfully, is no longer.

When it happened, I could not describe the exciting phenomenon I was experiencing, but I knew that the way I thought and how I had done things prior to 2002 were over and gone.

I felt alone in this new world without an adequate vocabulary and without many folks with whom to converse. At last, I have the right words—digital mindset—and the corresponding vocabulary, and sharing this information is the reason for this book.

It is such an exciting time. It makes me wish that my parents and grandparents had had this kind of excitement at this stage of their lives. And that they were here to experience the digital mindset.

—Carol Ingley

# The
# Digital
# Mindset

# Embrace Infinity

### The First Step

The digital mindset journey begins, as all journeys do, with a first step. That first step is, or so it may seem, awfully simple: Embrace infinity.

Infinity, as defined by *Merriam-Webster's Collegiate Dictionary*, is "boundlessness" or "an indefinitely great number or amount." Infinity is at the heart of the process of retooling and rewiring for the digital age. In other words, you will have to get your mind around the reality that the digital world is so vast that it goes beyond imagining. This vastness comes not just from the sheer quantity of information available online but also from the ability to mix and match digits in endless ways.

1

The concept of mixing and matching digits is integral to the digital mindset. With software, a single digital photograph can be altered endlessly. Digital text presentations can incorporate digital voice and digital video clips. A digital keyboard allows endless arrangements through the ability to mix and match digital tones, digital rhythms and digital notes. And, with more and more information coming online daily, there are boundless possibilities for creating digital content tailored just the way you want it to be.

Embracing this concept of infinity is slightly different from accepting it. To accept is more passive than to embrace. The digital mindset requires your active participation. The concept of infinity must be actively embraced.

You may, however, find yourself caught up in data overdrive rather than the excitement of all these possibilities. Sometimes when I think about infinity and all the possibilities of the digital age, my brain does little somersaults, anything to get away from the boundlessness of it all. If it doesn't do somersaults, then my brain seems to want to go on vacation. This is not awfully simple. It is simply awful. These are natural reactions to any complex concept.

It may take a leap of faith to embrace infinity as the foundation of a new way of thinking, but it is a necessary first step.

By embracing infinity, you have entered the digital mindset.

> Embrace infinity as the foundation
> of the digital mindset.
>
> Source: ingleyCONSULTANCY

## Payoff

There is a payoff to taking this first step of embracing infinity as the foundation of the digital mindset. You may believe that there are no real shortcuts in life, yet the digital mindset is about as close to a shortcut as you are going to get.

By taking this journey, you will be shortcutting frustration. You will be shortcutting anxiety. You will be shortcutting despair. You will be shortcutting disorientation. You will be shortcutting confusion. With the digital mindset, you will be able to navigate effectively the vast amount of digital information online. You will find that your life is much more manageable as a result. In fact, you will not only feel more in control of your life, you will *be* more in control of your life. You will become more proactive and less reactive. You will discover that, at the heart of your being, there is a feeling of excitement and energy that you would never have thought possible.

## Left Behind

Let's say that the idea of embracing infinity doesn't sound very believable to you. You may think that these promises are empty and that infinity sounds like meaningless jargon or, worse, meaningless jargon now targeted at the digital age. Infinity is, after all, a concept that has been around for a very long time. What if I told you that, if you do not embrace infinity as the foundation of the digital mindset, you will be left behind?

If you choose not to take this first step, sooner or later you will find yourself wandering around in a daze due to "circuit overload" from reading and going through mountains of digital data. You will be overwhelmed by a "to do" list that you can never quite manage. You will wonder not only why you cannot keep up, but why you are already exhausted and you are still not keeping up. You will notice that your job or career has been changing and you haven't been changing with it. You may also notice that your personal finances aren't working the way they used to. Maybe this is the position you already find yourself in.

Worse, you will begin to observe those around you who *are* keeping up. These folks will have already taken on the digital mindset and, rather than being "overworked," they are, instead, relaxed. But they're not just relaxed–they are excited about life. They will be managing tons of data, organizing it, understanding it, tapping into their creative talents, and finding plenty of time for everything they want to do. They will be able to shift from job to job with relative ease or, alternatively, start their own businesses.

Despite reading this, you still may not be convinced. You may say to yourself that, thus far, you have been plenty smart and things mostly go your way. That may be true for now, fleetingly, but, in three to five years, you will be left in the dust. At that time, you will see that taking on the digital mindset has become a necessity of life. You can shake off the dust at that time and begin recreating yourself by taking on this new perspective. By then, however, so many others will have already recreated themselves that you will be running after the bus, so to speak. Eventually, you may well catch up, but the journey will be painful indeed.

## History of Infinity

Simply defined, infinity can mean the useful concept of a process with no end.

Mathematicians, philosophers, and men of God have struggled with the concept of infinity for centuries.

It is thought that the Greeks discovered the idea of infinity. Early accounts of infinity come from Zeno of Elea, who lived around 490 BC. Other early cultures, including early India, embraced the concept as well. The *Isha Upanishad of the Yajurveda*, an ancient Hindu scripture, says that "if you remove a part from infinity or add a part to infinity, still what remains is infinity."

Other religions have dealt with the idea. The over-all concept of Christianity is based on the infinite love of God.

The idea of infinity, then, is not new. Nor is this the first time that the idea of infinity has been disconcerting. Back in 490 BC, the concept did not come easily to the Greeks. It is said to have caused pain, insanity and perhaps even murder.

Some may quibble about using the term *infinity* in the context of the digital age. It really doesn't matter whether you think of the digital age as infinite, endless, or very large and complex. What matters is taking on a digital world so vast that it must be managed in a new way.

The emergence of the importance of infinity in the digital age occurs at a unique moment of history. Thus, it is also a unique moment to take the plunge into a new way of thinking.

## Unique Moment in History

What makes this a unique moment in history? What makes this a moment when one should change?

This unique point in time is occurring because the major content categories—audio/video, data and voice—are now primarily digital. These digital content categories reflect the three major digital services: digital TV, broadband Internet, and voice, also known as the triple play.

---

The major content categories—audio/video, data and voice—are now primarily digital.

Source: ingleyCONSULTANCY

---

Keep in mind that these categories are not perfect. In fact, the cable TV industry calls the triple play video, data and voice. Since video refers to digital TV, video is more accurately described with the phrase audio/video given that TV is both video and audio. Audio/video is the term that will be used throughout this book.

All this shift to the triple play and digital content is quite recent. And it did not come easily,

In *Business Week*'s June 25, 2007, cover story entitled "Telecom Back from the Dead," the gory details of 2000 through 2007 are laid out. According to *Business Week*, the telecommunications industry was in 2000, "laid low by the worst collapse to hit a U.S. industry since the Great Depression." Companies large and small filed for bankruptcy. Shortly after the collapse of the telecom industry in 2000, the dot-com bubble burst.

What was going on behind the scenes had much to do with retooling for the digital age. This digital conversion was, indeed, a process of converting audio/video, data, and voice to a common standard of 1s and 0s, the language of the digital age. But it also involved a new way of corporate thinking.

If the telecom, information technology, and Internet industries had to retool, it stands to reason that you will need to retool as well.

---

The digital mindset requires that you
retool for the digital age.

Source: ingleyCONSULTANCY

---

## Audio/Video, Data and Voice: Shift to Digital

Computers are digital machines. Their primary language is digital: 1s and 0s. There are other types of data, of course, such as handwritten records of your personal finances. These handwritten records are not digital. However, plug the numbers into a Microsoft Excel spreadsheet and they become digital.

The 1s and 0s are known as "bits," and the unit of measurement for digital information is 1 byte or 8 bits. Here are the 8 bits (or 1 byte) that represent the letters A and B of the alphabet:

01000001 = A

01000010 = B

Beyond data, there are two other triple play categories: voice and audio/video. Voice (primarily phone) and audio/video (such as movies, TV programs, home video and radio programs) were developed using analog technology or waves. The issue with analog technology is that waves cannot be mixed and matched the way digits can. Analog technology is a good technology, but it lacks the flexibility of digits.

Let's take a closer look at voice and how this digital conversion has happened (and is happening). Much of voice has gone digital (or is going digital) from its origins as an analog technology. Analog is the voice technology dating back to Alexander Graham Bell and his first phone conversation. This digital conversion from analog has been pushed along by digital smart phones and voice over the Internet. Going from an analog voice to digital voice is a fairly simple process. The height of the analog wave is compared to a scale. This scale—from 0 to 256—is converted into bits and bytes. That's digital voice in a nutshell. Still, not all voice is digital. You will find that most residential landlines with traditional phone service are still analog. Moving into the digital age is an ongoing process.

The shift from analog audio/video to digital audio/video involves a slightly different process. This category is actually three in one: video, audio, and audio/video. Suppose you are standing in front of the White House with a digital camcorder and wish to record the event. Digital *video* is recorded on a hard disk, CD, or DVD using digital hardware in contrast to analog *video* which is recorded on film or on a VCR tape.

TV is the primary *audio/video* digital service. The last major hurdle in the United States to the digital age was successfully navigated through the conversion of over-the-air TV from analog to digital in 2009. Other types of TV are different. Satellite TV is already all digital and cable TV is still in the process of going digital through 2012.

You may be wondering where *audio* (e.g., radio) fits in. Because a digital TV signal is both audio and video, you may, in fact, have music channels as part of your pay TV package. In principle, a radio channel can do the same, although a radio station is not permitted by the Federal Communications Commission to transmit video signals. Radio is, however, going through its own transformation and may soon be quite different from what it is today. It has gone digital for some stations. Again, this is an ongoing process. Digital radio signals can be received if you purchase a digital radio (also known as an HD radio) or have a digital tuner. This process of converting to digital for the three major content categories is obviously not yet complete, but it is mostly there. With the conversion of over-the-air TV to digital, the United States has reached a "tipping point," as Malcolm Gladwell might say.

---

The transition to digital has reached the "tipping point" in the United States.

Source: ingleyCONSULTANCY

---

So, audio/video, data, and voice, the currency of the information age, are now primarily digital. The "coins" are either 1s or 0s and these "coins" can be mixed and matched in bytes (units of eight digits). You can stay within one type of content and mix and match just video. You can mix and match audio/video and data. Or you can mix and match voice bytes. Whatever combination you wish to make, you can do it as long as you abide by copyright laws.

---

Mixing and matching digits can be seen as creating and putting together audio/video, data, and voice bytes in innovative, different, and novel ways.

Source: ingleyCONSULTANCY

---

## Digital Hardware "Married" with Digital Content

Hardware has also gone digital. There are now digital TVs, digital cameras, digital camcorders, digital phones, to name only a few of the digital devices. Marry these devices with digital audio/video, data, and voice and you can see that there has been a "retooling" of devices alongside the information that is shown, played, transmitted or aired on them: the content.

What, though, do these 1s and 0s mean? An understanding of these 1s and 0s is critical to knowing why infinity has to be the foundation of the digital mindset.

## 1s and 0s

When audio/video, data and voice are all digital, it means that they speak the same language—the language of 1s and 0s.

The digital rule is, then, all digital content speaks the same language.

---

The Digital Rule: All digital content
speaks the same language.

Source: ingleyCONSULTANCY

---

Said another way, a byte is a byte is a byte.

## A byte is a byte is a byte.

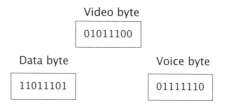

Source: ingleyCONSULTANCY

So what, you may ask. The world's knowledge is finite, and certainly not all of it is available online or in digital form elsewhere. You are right. Even if every speck of the world's knowledge could suddenly be available online, that would be a finite universe.

But because that knowledge is all digital and because digital audio/video, digital data, and digital voice all speak the same language, non-copyrighted fragments of Web sites, articles, newspapers, books, video, and voice can be mixed and matched in new and innovative ways. Content that you generate can be mixed and matched as well. Ideas formulated from diverse data points be mixed and matched. How many ways can information and ideas be mixed and matched? This mixing and matching of digits can be done in so many ways that it can be seen as infinite.

A set of digital photographs from a recent vacation can be taken as an example. You can take subsets of the photographs and add text. The text that you add can vary in endless ways. As already mentioned, you can alter one single photograph in endless ways. You can add video or voice to the photographs. You probably see where this is going. And this is just one set of digital photographs.

If one were to write on separate pieces of paper an explanation of each variation of this mixing and matching, stacked that paper in piles, those piles of paper would completely fill the emptiness of space and more.

Yet there's more to the concept of infinity than digital content.

## Infinity and Bandwidth

Sending and receiving digital information is where the power of the digital age lies. The backbone of the digital age is a network of pipes—also known as the information highway—that carries digital information to and from your "home." Home can be seen as your actual home, an office, a boat, an automobile, or any other place.

---

Backbone of the Digital Age:
The backbone of the digital age is
a network of pipes—also known as the
digital highway—that carries digital
information to and from your home.

Source: ingleyCONSULTANCY

---

Fiber optics, a technology that is now becoming available into the home, is characterized as a technology with almost infinite bandwidth. Technology hasn't evolved to even begin to take full advantage of that capability, but, by understanding fiber optics' true capabilities, one can see ahead.

What, then, lies ahead? If you have fiber optics coming into your home, then you have almost infinite bandwidth. But only a portion of fiber-optic capabilities are available to you via the services being offered by the carrier or owner of the fiber-optic network. Much of it is unused and unavailable to you. Right now, the primary services are digital TV, broadband Internet, and voice, but these services are set to change in order to fill the pipes, so to speak. Other technologies such as the cable into the home that currently carries the triple play of digital TV, broadband Internet, and voice work in similar ways, but do not have quite the power of fiber optics.

The world is moving, then, toward infinite content and almost infinite bandwidth to send and receive content.

Let's say some of what is being discussed is starting to convince you at least to *try on* this new idea of infinity.

## Trying on New Lenses

Embracing infinity as the foundation of the digital mindset is like trying on a new pair of glasses when you didn't even know you needed them. Suddenly, you see the world in an entirely different way. Everything comes into focus. Embracing infinity is putting life in a new focus and a new light. It will allow you to see everything from a new perspective.

## Unleashing of Constraints

With these new lenses on, you may begin to see that although the world worked well before becoming "digitized," its technologies constrained the possibility of change on a grand scale. You couldn't mix and match very easily. Now, you can take those digits and with the proper knowledge and software, create your own videos, video resumes, podcasts, blogs, video blogs, digital scrapbooks, and digital photo albums. The list goes on and on—and it is just the beginning.

The unleashing of constraints affects the digital side of your life and your life in general. With the digital mindset, every category of life becomes unconstrained.

One way in which life's categories show this "lack of constraint" is the blurring of boundaries and overlapping of categories. For example, the boundary between work and play has already become less clear, as has the boundary between home and office. These are general life categories.

Looking more directly at the digital side of life, characteristics and capabilities of a smart phone are overlapping the PC and now, slowly, the digital TV. The PC is overlapping the characteristics of digital TV and the smart phone. The digital TV is starting to overlap PC and smart phone characteristics.

This unleashing of constraints doesn't mean that suddenly all your dreams will come true. It does mean, however, that you will have more control, not less, in achieving those dreams.

Despite this control, it may make you tired just thinking about all this change and this "unleashing of constraints." It is a challenge to take this on. And it is the first step that is the hardest.

Before beginning, let's see where it is all headed.

## Where It Is All Headed

Luckily, there is an end in sight. This end will always be your guide, a map so to speak, but only a map with a destination point I call the digital endgame. The digital endgame is that any digital device will be able to send and receive digital audio/video, data, and voice. All digital devices will be able to connect to a network. This network could be in your home, an office, a boat, an automobile, or any other place.

---

The Digital Endgame: Any digital device will be able to send and receive digital audio/video, data, and voice. All digital devices will be able to connect to a network.

Source: ingleyCONSULTANCY

---

Where everything is headed is more than this, though.

## Simplicity

A core concept of the digital mindset is simplicity. It might sound contradictory in the face of the complexities of high-tech, but actually it makes sense. Faced with the infinite possibilities of mixing and matching digital content, anyone who can come up with simple answers amidst all the complexities of infinity will be a winner.

Think of being at a dinner party or an office meeting and someone talks on and on, revealing detail upon arcane detail to you. When the monologue is over, you are ready to fall asleep.

Now, contrast that with someone who makes the complex appear simple. That person shakes the cobwebs from the obscure and makes it clear. The kind of ideas presented can save you time and money. They sound exciting.

If you can make the complex clear and simple, you will find that your relationships, work life and home life are different. You will be needed in a way that you have never been needed before.

The steps to taking on the digital mindset—ten in total—will lead you to simplicity.

But, for the moment, let's return to certain complexities of the digital age.

## O'Dell's Law

Mike O'Dell, an Internet guru, created a law in the late 1990s: If you're not scared, you don't understand. The law refers to the vast, impending changes that were headed toward high-tech industries at that time. A few years later, the bottom fell out of the telecommunications industry. Then the dot-com bubble burst.

And although O'Dell's law was intended for the business community, it really now applies to you and me.

O'Dell does not suggest that you make decisions out of fear. But a little bit of fear to get someone moving is not necessarily bad.

If you're not at least a little bit scared, then you don't understand!

Okay, you don't want to take this journey out of fear. You really want to take this journey because it will lead you to a fun, exciting, and fulfilling life.

Now let's look at the biggest payoff of all.


## The Biggest Payoff of All

There just might be a little voice inside you thinking that, if the digital mindset is all about infinity, maybe, just maybe, anything is possible after all.

With the digital mindset, anything is possible. . . and "anything" can happen more quickly.

---

With the digital mindset, anything is possible.

Source: ingleyCONSULTANCY

---

The digital mindset does not let you make excuses. You are now in the driver's seat. The biggest payoff of all is that you can make anything happen.

Well, what are you waiting for? Let's go!

## Making the Shift
## to Embracing Infinity

Making the shift to embrace infinity is a decision. It may actually be, for you, a line in the sand. It may also happen subliminally as you tacitly rearrange your life to accommodate this concept.

You might wish to consider what Bill Gates used to do on an annual basis while he was CEO of Microsoft. He would take a retreat. You may not have the week or two that he invested in this process, but you can take a walk. If these concepts are new to you, you may wish to consider blocking out time for a long walk. This could even be a three-hour walk—long enough to be able to clear your head and contemplate this journey. It could be a day or weekend retreat to a cabin or a robust bike ride. Whatever you choose, it is best to do it by yourself. This is *your* journey.

Part of this journey is about practice. Practice the thought of infinity. Infinity is your new sandbox, and it changes everything.

There is a well-known quote from U.S. Supreme Court Justice Potter Stewart who, in trying to define hard-core pornography in 1964, knew that he could not find the right words, but wrote instead, "I know it when I see it." His words have become famous and are quoted often.

You will know infinity when you embrace it. You will know because your perspective about everything will change.

Here are some questions to ask yourself.

1.  What does infinity mean to me?

    *My answer:* Infinity has been my sandbox since
    October 2002. At that time, I figured out that
    every "tool" that I used in my consulting and
    forecasting business was too dull for use in the
    digital age. Examining past trends to predict fu-
    ture trends was not going to work the way it had
    in the past. Even current trends had to be ex-
    amined in a new light. The "infinity" component
    of the digital age threw everything into disar-
    ray until, gradually, I began to take on the digi-
    tal mindset. I now look at trends in a "mix and
    match" fashion, much like mixing and matching
    1s and 0s. At times, it has been scary to confront
    so much change, because infinity is so big and so
    variable! Overall, though, it makes me incred-
    ibly excited to be alive. I also know that as I em-
    brace infinity and understand how to manage it,
    my life becomes more and more interesting. Ex-
    periencing this process has allowed me to write
    this book. I have more opportunities, not fewer.
    My dreams get bigger, not smaller.

2.  The digital age is characterized by the unleash-
    ing of constraints. What does that mean to me
    and how does it affect me?

    *My answer:* Personally, this unleashing affects
    me every day. Some days, I revert to old ways.
    One old way is not making organization a top
    priority. Organization is an important part of

the digital mindset that will be discussed later in more detail (see Step 5). Sometimes I get caught up in the frustrations of life. Sometimes I forget about all the possibilities because I get so busy. Almost every day, I try to remind myself to apply the digital mindset to everything I do. It is not yet natural, and I do have to remind myself. But when I get back on track and am using all aspects of the digital mindset, ideas flow in a way they never have before. In fact, all my life flows much more effortlessly when I embrace these concepts. It is exhilarating.

3. What if I am resisting this change about embracing infinity? Should I go on a retreat?

*My answer:* It is natural to be resistant here. This is a change of perspective that will affect all aspects of your life. As a telecommunications consultant in the 1990s, I saw some big changes coming, but I didn't quite understand the implications. So, in 1995, when it looked like broadband (or fast) Internet connections would be the wave of the future, I took a retreat. At the time, narrowband (dial-up or slow) connections to the Internet were the norm. I stayed a week in the Williamsburg, Virginia, area and decided not to speak with anyone, other than to order food at restaurants and tour Colonial Williamsburg. Mostly, as I remember, I didn't talk. It was an internal journey about the future, so I brought items to read that I thought might be helpful. This retreat affected my life positively. It was a first step toward the digital mindset. Primarily as a result of this week, the focus of my business later shifted to broadband and ultimately led to the concepts presented in this book.

# Leverage Infinity

One characteristic of embracing infinity is that you have now taken on the big picture. There is no bigger picture than infinity.

De facto, you are now a big picture kind of person. Of course, the temptation may be to just stop here, embrace infinity, and be good to go.

Not so fast. Let's take a look at what's happening around you. The University of Phoenix advertises that 20 million articles are available to its students online. And that's in 2010. Who knows what that number may be in three to five years? Count on it doubling or tripling. The University of California at Berkeley's library has a goal: Get all of the library's collection online. Amazon Chairman and CEO Jeff Bezos has stated that he wants all books available online to Kindle users. *All books!*

Everywhere you look, there are plans to put offline information online. There must be a way to navigate through this. Because you now are a big-picture player, what is the next step?

The next step is to leverage infinity. You can do that in any number of ways.

## The Appropriate Big Picture

Now that your sandbox is huge, how are you going to play in it? Another core concept of the digital mindset is the ability to solve problems, issues, and dilemmas on your own.

---

A core concept of the digital mindset is the ability to solve problems, issues, and dilemmas on your own.

Source: ingleyCONSULTANCY

---

Something you may want to solve is how to achieve a goal or dream that you have. Laura Day says in *How to Rule the World from Your Couch*, "Ask yourself, Who do you wish to be? And don't judge yourself on the response, whether it's 'I wish to be beautiful' or 'I wish to be more powerful.'"

To solve these issues or problems or to achieve a goal or dream, you need to cut infinity down to size.

What is that size? That size, ironically, is another big picture, a subset of infinity. In other words, to leverage infinity, you must define the appropriate big picture.

---

To leverage infinity, you must define the appropriate big picture.

Source: ingleyCONSULTANCY

---

What does that really mean? Some practical examples should help clarify this idea. Suppose you are either changing jobs or are new to the job market. Thus, you are trying to achieve a goal of finding a new job. To actually find a job, you will need to ask many questions. Your first question should be the biggest one, however. What kind of big picture question might you ask?

Here's a possibility: What is the global market for this prospective position?

This question puts your prospective job in the biggest picture possible: the entire world.

Let's say that you specialize in software development. What countries have software developers in abundance, and what do these developers charge per hour? You'll need to know more than just an hourly labor rate. Specifically, you will need to know what rate is charged to U.S. companies by foreign contracting firms. In other words, if a U.S. company hires a contracting firm from India, what is the corporate rate charged? The world is *not* flat from this perspective. A flat world would have similar labor rates wherever you went. Rather, the world is round for labor rates and they vary in different countries around the world.

Once you have determined rates in countries with large numbers of software developers, your next question might be: Now that the rates are known, what is my rate?

You probably think in terms of salary. Salary is important but what is your rate? If you are potentially competing against others who do have a known hourly rate, you had better know your own. Let's say that the salary you want is $60,000. There are 52 weeks in a year and 40 hours per work week. That's a total of 2,080 hours that you want to be paid for working. Benefits and other costs to the employer also need to be included. These costs vary and can be quite high if items such as overhead are included. Let's use a conservative 30%. Because 30% of $60,000 is $18,000, the real pay that you are interested in is $78,000. If you divide $78,000 by 2,080, you will find your rate. It is $37.50 per hour.

You are competing in a global market at a rate of $37.50 per hour.

Some jobs at such firms as snow removal companies, landscape companies, cleaning companies and other types of local services do not compete in the global job market. Or, at least, so it seems.

Yet there really are no truly local companies anymore. Snow removal companies, landscape companies, and cleaning companies need logos, Web sites, mailers, and brochures. Some of these tasks can be outsourced to the least expensive company, and that might be outside the United States.

Another big picture question might be: Where is China going to be in five to ten years? That's quite a big picture question. To answer it, you will have to look at many areas: social, economic, political, philosophical, geographic, moral, and so forth. You will need historical information, current information, and information about the immediate future. And that is just the beginning of a list of the areas into which you will have to delve if you choose to explore this kind of big picture question.

As you begin to leverage infinity, you will see that all kinds of things can be now seen as big picture.

## Big Picture But How Big?

The size of the big picture will vary according to any issue or problem that you want solved. The bigger the net you throw, the more valuable your answers will be. In other words, the bigger the question you ask, the bigger the answers. If you truly take on where China will be in five to ten years, it is likely that you will be able to find niches for a business or write a book that will be helpful to those wishing to do business in China. You may end up on CNN, NBC, or the radio. As another example, if you study future trends of the Internet, cable TV, satellite TV, over-the-air TV, broadband, voice, interactive TV and so forth, you may see relationships among the categories that otherwise would be easy to miss.

---

The bigger the net you throw, the more
valuable your answers will be.

Source: ingleyCONSULTANCY

---

## Play a Game That's Stacked Against You

If you are an ambitious player in the digital world, you
will want to leverage infinity in such a way that you
are playing a game that's stacked against you.

---

To leverage infinity powerfully, play a
game that's stacked against you.

Source: ingleyCONSULTANCY

---

Playing a game that's stacked against you is looking
at a bigger picture than you would ever have dreamed
possible. It is a variation of the business principle of
the bigger the risk, the bigger the reward.

The bigger net you throw, the bigger the reward.

### Ask a Lot of Questions

Even with a big picture that has cut infinity down to
size, you will now have to cut that big picture down to
size. You can do so by asking a lot of questions.

You may wish to start with a list. Once you have
your list, or the beginnings of a list, you may want to
stop for the day. It is important to stop before you get
tired and a little before you have completed the list.

When you get back to your list, you will find that it is quite easy to continue. You may see that you are finished writing down questions and are ready to get answers. In the end, it may not be a list of questions per se. It could be an outline.

> You leverage infinity by asking a lot of questions. Stop before you get tired.
>
> Source: ingleyCONSULTANCY

Now the adventure begins.

## Not All Who Wander Are Lost

Let's say that you've found your big picture issue, have made a list of bite-size questions, and are now plugging those questions into your Web browser or a search engine. You are starting to get some interesting answers, but some of those answers are pulling you in a slightly different direction than you anticipated. You will have to make the decision whether to go that new way.

Keep in mind that not all who wander are lost. Wandering is an important component of the digital mindset, and it is a way to leverage infinity.

> You can leverage infinity by wandering.
>
> Source: ingleyCONSULTANCY

## Your Life as a Big Picture

The digital mindset and its orientation toward the big picture changes your perspective about everything, not just regarding digital information. You begin to see everything from this big picture perspective. For example, you can view your home as a big picture. Managing a home is more complex in the digital age, so seeing your home as a big picture is helpful. Let's say that you want to manage your money better and have now taken on the big picture of your home and its expense. You may see that there are areas that need constant maintenance. For example, furniture does not take constant maintenance other than cleaning. Replenishing food in your kitchen, however, does take constant maintenance. These constant maintenance areas of your home might be classified into seven categories: kitchen, bathroom, closet, digital assets, personal grooming, transportation, and health. If your home has different needs, you can amend the categories. If you have a yard, for instance, that would require constant maintenance. You may want to add in entertainment, but that is not an area that needs constant maintenance; it is more an icing on the cake kind of category. (By adding in entertainment, however, you may find out that's where your money is going!) Through taking on this particular big picture, you can get a better handle on how you are spending your money on the constant maintenance areas of your home.

This example is presented because you cannot begin to see digital information as divvied up into different big pictures and big picture questions without beginning to categorize the rest of your life in terms of big pictures.

By taking on the biggest picture of all–infinity–you get used to seeing the world as a big picture. One big picture leads to another.

---

### With the digital mindset, one big picture leads to another.

Source: ingleyCONSULTANCY

---

## Mixing and Matching

The ability to mix and match is one of the most powerful elements of the digital mindset. This is not just about mixing and matching digits. It is also about mixing and matching concepts. The mixing and matching of concepts is made easier given the enormous amount of information available online.

---

### The process of mixing and matching is an effective way to leverage infinity.

Source: ingleyCONSULTANCY

---

Returning to the example of China's future, it is possible to compare the future of China with the future of India. It is likely that valuable information will be found in this comparison using the mixing and matching principle.

Let's say you choose two parameters: population and geography. If you think that there is more to population and geography than meets the eye, you will be on the lookout for a different angle. If you continue to ask that sort of question, particularly in comparing the two countries, you will stay the course in your search for valuable information. Certain questions come to mind: What about the future population of China and India is similar? What about the future population of China and India is different? What are the implications of China and India being geographically close to each other? How does geography play a role in their economies? As you progress through reading and Web search questions, your own questions will become more refined.

In addition, many companies are thinking of investing in one, the other or both of these countries, a trend you will likely stumble upon or learn during your research. Or you can leverage your knowledge by contacting these companies at a later date.

## Digital Information as the Great Equalizer

To leverage infinity effectively, you will have to accept that digital information is the great equalizer.

If you are counting on the status quo to get you where you want to go, that's so 1990s. Just think about what the phrase *status quo* means: the existing state of affairs.

The status quo is not something most people think about. They do not realize that it is, in fact, a mindset. Right now, it is still the prevailing mindset in the United States.

In a way, the digital mindset and its ramifications can be compared to the revolution of thought that occurred when the printing press was invented. Suddenly, books that were only available to the most scholarly or the wealthiest were commonplace.

Because the United States was built on the premise of personal freedom, the right to design your own life, and the ability to achieve your dreams, the digital mindset fits into the existing core value template. One might hypothesize that what is holding back the United States now in getting through the current economic times is a thought pattern that no longer works. That thought pattern is status quo thinking, and that thought pattern no longer helps Americans fulfill their core value template.

In the digital world, the existing state of affairs changes and gets reinvented often, sometimes daily. Thus, any existing state of affairs is transitory at best.

The digital mindset becomes the new status quo through the ability to leverage infinity. This new status quo equalizes everyone.

---

You cannot leverage infinity without understanding
that digital information is the great equalizer.

Source: ingleyCONSULTANCY

---

It is important to keep this in mind because competition is now global as a result of the universality of the digital mindset. It is a constant reminder that you will not be able to rest on your laurels. That's the bad news. The good news is that if you have a strategy in place in your life whereby you are leveraging infinity effectively, you will feel secure about the many opportunities you will encounter in your journey.

## Old Media Versus New Media

Leveraging infinity is not just about new media that is in the form of digits. It is also about old media.

---

Leverage infinity by taking on both old media and new media.

Source: ingleyCONSULTANCY

---

The categories of old media versus new media tend to fall into paper or analog technologies as old media and online or digitally stored information as new media.

Make note that the world is now—and will continue to be—both old media and new media. Each has its role with the digital mindset. Leveraging infinity means making use of both old and new media.

| Old Media | New Media |
|---|---|
| Books | Online books |
| Newspapers | Online newspapers |
| Photographs | Digital photographs |
| Video from analog camcorder | Video from digital camcorder |
| Analog voice | Digital voice |
| Analog TV | Digital TV |
| Analog games | Digital games |
| Analog radio | Digital radio |

## Leveraging Time

As exciting as it is to have infinity at one's fingertips, it may be humbling to discover that not all your resources are infinite. One finite resource is time. For all your efforts, you will have ultimately more free time, not less. The digital mindset is not about overbooking yourself. It is about a process that allows you to streamline your life.

You will have more time to have fun, but your definition of fun will change. It will be intermingled with learning in a new and exciting way.

In 1968, Andy Warhol said, "In the future, everyone will be world famous for 15 minutes."

Beyond your 15 minutes of fame—prophetically quite possible for everyone due to the Internet—the information age changes just that: 15 minutes.

Those pockets of 15 minutes, in the digital age, are precious. You can leverage these short time frames.

Are these pockets of 15 minutes important because your time is so jammed with activity that 15 minutes is all the time you have?

No, that's not the reason for leveraging pockets of 15 minutes. The reason for leveraging 15 minutes is that because you have access to so much information, a lot can be accomplished in a very short period of time.

See for yourself. Use the big picture methodology to start and create a set of questions. Devote 15 minutes a day to it for a month. You will see that the progress that you make is amazing.

You will begin to see that you have 15 minutes of fame every day!

---

Leverage time by using those pockets
of 15 minutes every day.

Source: ingleyCONSULTANCY

---

Once you begin to value those small pockets of time, you will likely have little tolerance for letting your time be wasted. You will begin to view time as the precious commodity it is.

The trade-off is that you must be willing to be engaged in the process of acquiring the digital mindset, to take the process on as though your life depended upon it. And, in a strange sort of way, it does.

## Core Values

Leveraging infinity becomes rather empty if it is not done with a backdrop of values. As society changes, values change with it. A new set of core values emerges with the digital mindset. Some of these values are: education, global marketplace, new respect for the individual, trust (particularly trust in oneself), multiple career track, connection and the new heroism. They are familiar concepts but they must be adapted for the digital mindset. Then, they can be leveraged. Obviously, values in the digital age will differ from individual to individual, and this is just a sample list. And you might take issue about whether the global marketplace and a multiple career track are really values anyway. In a sense, they are. There must be a shift to where you value the world as a market and where you value taking a multiple career track for you to stay up-to-date with the digital age. With social media and messaging such as e-mailing and texting, connection is constant, broader and more diverse than it has been in the past. All of this connection means that respect and trust become more valued. The new heroism has yet to be defined. The old heroism definition of saving lives and helping others in dramatic ways still exists. As the world gets more peaceful and the roles less traditional, however, a new definition needs to emerge.

For a specific example of core values in the digital age, consider education. You likely value it already. It is considered one of the keys to success in the United States. Suddenly, with the movie *Waiting for Superman*, there is a great deal of attention being focused on making education better in the United States. This attention is related to the digital mindset. Education, in fact, *has* to change. Teaching students how to think with the digital mindset is critical. It is about learning and thinking in a new way.

With the digital mindset, education takes on a heightened value for all ages. It needs to be incorporated into one's daily life, rather than occurring in phases such as grade school, high school, undergraduate school, graduate school and courses that one takes along the way. Education is a way to deal with a core concept of the digital age, and that is constant change. One way to incorporate education into your life is to learn something new about your digital assets every day. Believe it or not, 365 new ways of doing things adds up over the year and makes a huge difference.

---

Leverage core values.

Source: ingleyCONSULTANCY

---

## Making the Shift to Leveraging Infinity

Making the shift to leveraging infinity means thinking in terms of big pictures. The next step is to add questions or an outline to the big picture.
Here are some questions to ask yourself.

1. What are some current "big pictures" in my life?

   *My answer:* One "big picture" in my life are the pockets of 15 minutes that I find I have daily. Although I go through cycles, I try to use these pockets to do genealogy research on my family. Online research is phenomenal, not to mention the joy of finding long-lost distant cousins. Online research has allowed me to create booklets of family history for Christmas gifts. I have also digitized early photos that I like and am creating mini photo albums by rearranging the pictures. In addition, those pockets of 15 minutes have come in handy as I relearn how to play the piano using a digital keyboard.

2. How do I use both old media and new media in my life?

   *My answer:* I love being able to intermingle both old media and new media. I have subscriptions to trade and other types of magazines. Reading them on paper rather than online works better for me, although I do both.

3. What are my fears about leveraging infinity and taking on constant change?

   *My answer:* At first, I thought that dealing with constant change would take away any extra time that I had. In the beginning, when I was getting the hang of it, it was very demanding timewise. But now I see that I can manage my time much better even though I am processing ten times more information. I also thought that I would have to sacrifice my sense of humanity. It turns out to be quite the opposite. I can be just as feeling and compassionate a person, but now logic plays a larger role.

# Rewire Your Brain to the Digital Mindset

Do the concepts of embracing infinity and leveraging infinity just discussed seem to do strange things to your mind? To deal with infinity and leverage infinity, I have had to rewire my brain. You will, too, if you haven't already.

The digital mindset requires "rewiring" the brain.

Source: ingleyCONSULTANCY

To rewire the brain, we need to understand how it is currently wired. But first, is this trip really necessary? Why rewire the brain?

## Why Rewire?

Rewiring the brain is necessary because you may not be using all your brain power.

You may have seen it on YouTube (search on "Spinning Lady"). It is a spinning silhouette of a lady.

It looks like the silhouette of a lady is spinning either clockwise or counterclockwise. To me, it looks like she is spinning clockwise. To others, she will look like she is spinning counterclockwise. Some will be able to switch back and forth and see both.

This is not a spinning lady video but rather a video of a lady moving back and forth very quickly. Whether you see it spinning one way or the other depends on the dominance of the right side or the left side of your brain.

This exercise becomes important because the digital mindset requires that you use your whole brain. Most of us prefer to use that part of the brain that is easiest to access.

If you see the lady spinning clockwise, you tend to be right-brained. Alternatively, if you see the lady spinning counterclockwise, you tend to be left-brained. Being able to switch back and forth to see both indicates that you use both sides of your brain.

The spinning lady exercise is presented here to get you thinking about which side of the brain you tend to use. And remember that this left-brain and right-brain experiment is only about the cerebral cortex–just one part of the brain.

So, to understand how to use the whole brain, an understanding of its complex nature and its parts is in order.

## Understanding the Structure of the Brain

Structurally, the brain is not that complicated, but a few terms need to be defined. There are four major parts of the human brain that will be examined here:

- Cerebral cortex, left hemisphere
- Cerebral cortex, right hemisphere
- Brain stem
- Cerebellum

## Cerebral Cortex: Left and Right Hemispheres

The cerebral cortex has two parts: a left hemisphere and a right hemisphere. As the spinning lady demonstrated, people tend to be left-brained or right-brained, whichever side of the cerebral cortex tends to be dominant.

In general, left-handed people are right-brained and right-handed people are left-brained. Left-handed people—right-brained in general—tend to be more intuitive and right-handed people—left-brained in general—tend to be more logical and rational. Just keep that in mind.

In general, the right side of your brain controls the left side of your body and the left side of your brain controls the right side of your body. Here there is some symmetry. But beyond this symmetry of controlling two different sides of the body, the two sides of the brain have different specialties.

The left brain functions in a logical fashion. It controls number skills, written language skills, analytical skills, rational thinking skills, objective skills and the ability to think in terms of parts of the whole.

The right brain functions quite differently and is the side of imagination, music, intuition, art awareness as well as an ability to take seemingly random objects and synthesize them into an order that makes sense. The right brain sees the whole versus the parts.

To recap, the left brain is logical, sequential, rational, analytical, objective and it looks at parts. The right brain is random, intuitive, holistic, synthesizing, subjective, and it looks at wholes.

Having just discussed the "big picture" aspect of the digital mindset, you can see that it has right-brain elements because it looks at wholes.

Part of the digital mindset, however, must put together a series of questions or a process that looks at parts. And although some of these questions may be intuitive, there is a part of the brain that must work in a sequential, rational, analytical and objective fashion, all characteristics of the left brain.

## Brain Stem:
## The Oldest Part of the Brain

The oldest part of the brain is the brain stem. It evolved hundreds of millions of years ago and is often referred to as the reptilian brain because reptiles have brains similar to the brain stem. The brain stem is at the core of the brain and its power cannot be overestimated. Thus, the brain stem is also known as the control center. It controls basic emotions such as love, hate, fear, lust and contentment and basic life functions such as heart rate, breathing and the fight or flight response.

You cannot "rewire" the brain stem *directly*. Some control mechanisms of the brain stem cannot be tampered with at all. You cannot change your heart rate or the way your breathing works. You can over-ride breathing temporarily by holding your breath, but eventually the brain stem's control kicks in automatically.

Even so, in certain circumstances, the brain stem can be impacted *indirectly*. This indirect influence on the brain stem is an important part of the digital mindset and is discussed below under the heading "A Workhorse of the Digital Mindset."

## Cerebellum

The cerebellum is known to control reflexes, balance, and coordination. It sits on top of the brain stem, "a baseball-sized, bean shaped lump of gray and white brain tissue," according to Ray S. Snider in an issue of *Scientific American* in 1958.

Little is understood about this part of the brain. Given that it has increased threefold in size over the past million years of human evolution, it is theorized that it must be playing an important role. Yet if the cerebellum is removed from young children, it seems to have little effect on them.

Could there be a much larger role for the cerebellum, such as a living backup system? Because so little is known about the cerebellum, it will remain in the distant background of the digital mindset. If it does turn out to be some sort of living backup system for the rest of the brain, it may be that humans are more computer-like than realized. Or perhaps computers are more like the brain.

The parts of the brain that are most important for the digital mindset, then, are the left and right hemispheres of the cerebral cortex and the brain stem.

## Intermingling of Skills

So what does brain anatomy have to do with the digital mindset? Just reading the first part of this book may have given you some clues. Dealing with infinity is tough with only logical and rational skills or only intuitive, creative skills. It takes imagination to envision boundlessness. At the same time, reasoning and logical skills are needed to cut the big picture down to size.

In other words, the digital mindset must be able to absorb large amounts of information and be able to make sense of it all. This synthesizing, looking at the whole, and intuitive part of the learning process using the right side of the brain is as important as the logical and rational skills you use when looking at this information using the left side of the brain.

The skills from the two sides can be intermingled. If you use those logical and rational skills from the left side of the brain to begin to organize the data, then you can begin to tap into the right side of the brain to synthesize data and see it as a whole. You can also apply the imagination skills from the right side of the brain to come up with creative ideas about the information at hand.

In the digital world, you are dealing with vast amounts of information. It seems clear that finding that information takes rational, objective skills. Organizing the information may also take those same rational, objective skills. Using the information effectively, however, will require skills from the other side of the brain.

The digital mindset means that you really cannot focus only on one side of the brain.

---

The digital mindset means that you cannot
focus only on one side of the brain.

Source: ingleyCONSULTANCY

---

If—before the deluge of data that you now face—it worked to use just one side of your brain, now it can seem half-brained. Sorry! You will need to learn to move back and forth between the two sides of the brain. For some projects or endeavors, you may be using both seamlessly without being aware of it. You wouldn't necessarily know unless you make a conscious effort to observe it.

You would be surprised at how many famous rational, logical thinkers may actually have been using both sides of the brain. One of the most famous "rational" thinkers is Albert Einstein. Yet, if you read about him, it doesn't take long to find out that he was greatly influenced by a dream he had when he was very young. He noted later in life that his own life's work was based on trying to explain that dream. Therefore, elements of the imagination and intuition played a large role in his life, not to mention his integrated whole approach to physics.

Perhaps my own struggle with balancing the left and right sides of my brain is worthy to recount here. In 1990, I made the decision to leave the corporate world as a full-time executive to write a novel. This process was going to take me about a year as the rough draft was already complete. To support myself, I started a consulting practice. The plan was to return to a corporate position after a year.

What I found was that it takes much longer than a year to write a really good fiction book. I also discovered that I couldn't write fiction and consult at the same time. So, by choice, I would consult for a few months and then write fiction. Eventually, I took those writing skills and began to write and sell market studies in my consulting firm. The growth of the consulting business meant that I spent more time consulting and less time writing fiction. Still, I kept going and would always spend at least a few months a year devoted to fiction writing.

The point is that one may not be able use both skills seamlessly or simultaneously. Deliberately switching back and forth may be the best approach, and that takes practice. A more integrated approach using both the left and the right sides of the brain requires a personal evolution.

By the way, writing fiction is not just a right-brained, creative endeavor. Much of writing fiction entails research, a left-brain activity. You will find that many authors of fiction will say that research is the part of the writing process that they enjoy the most. That's because moving into the right brain means giving up the kind of control one feels on the left side of the brain. Neither is writing market and finance studies only a left-brain (logical and rational skills) activity. The ability to synthesize and make observations about vast amounts of data that others have overlooked is a right-brain activity.

Right-brain activity can be very draining for me. It would not be unusual for me, if it were a right-brain day, to be writing nonfiction or fiction (both can be right-brain activities, in my view) at a very early hour, say 5 a.m. The writing may be flowing. Hey, I'm probably feeling pretty good about that. I take time out for breakfast and then return to writing. Finally, I hit the wall. I am exhausted. I look at the clock. It is only 9 a.m.! Now what do I do with the rest of the day? These are some of the complications of using both sides of the brain. One side may peter out and it is likely to be the right-brain side (although everyone is different).

The rest of the day—for me—would have to consist of left-brain activities because my right brain is depleted for the day.

Other people have different experiences. I once attended a writers' conference where there was a panel of screenwriters. One screenwriter told a story of being in a meeting with Hollywood executives regarding the screenplay adaptation from a work of fiction. One of the executives turned to him and asked, "I hate to push like this, but can you get the screenplay to us in two weeks?" The writer solemnly promised that he could deliver. He was a fast writer and already knew the book. Unbeknownst to anyone but himself, he polished it off in three to four days. Given the fee that he was being paid, he thought it unwise to deliver early. So, he appeared, appropriately disheveled, after two weeks and, wiping his brow, delivered the goods. The point is that using the creative side of your brain doesn't have to be that hard.

For those definitively right-brained and feeling kind of cocky at the moment, hold on. Many artists and others who rely on their creative talents are very rusty when it comes to the left side of the brain. Give them a simple math problem involving percentages and they might not be able to solve it. In fact, they may just turn off their brain (or, at least, that side of the brain) when any quantitative explanation passes their way.

It take some conscious effort—a decision really—to use both sides of the brain. As my personal example showed, the decision to use both sides of the brain is not that easy. It requires an acknowledgment that the shift between the two may not be seamless. You may choose to have right-brain days and left-brain days.

---

Using both sides of the brain effectively
requires a conscious effort.

Source: ingleyCONSULTANCY

---

There is another perspective regarding being right-brained or being left-brained. It's whether you are male or female.

## Male Thinking Versus Female Thinking

It is politically correct to say that there really isn't any difference between male thinking and female thinking. Maybe it is true in some sense, yet male and female brains seem to be wired slightly differently.

As a generalization, women tend to use the right side of the brain more often than men. And they often underuse the left side of the brain.

The opposite is true with men, as a generalization. They tend to use the left side of the brain more often than women and often underuse the right

A man telling a woman that her intuitive viewpoint doesn't make any sense in lieu of the facts is a cliche. It is a classic example of left-brain, rational and logical thinking coming into conflict (rather than in balance) with right-brain thinking.

Because the digital mindset requires the use of both sides of the brain, rewiring the brain is going to be a challenge for both sexes. As a generalization, men will have to become more familiar with the right side of their brains and women will have to be more diligent about the left side of theirs.

## A Workhorse of the Digital Mindset

The digital mindset is about infinity, so you will need one of its workhorses to handle the data overload.

One workhorse of the digital mindset is the unconscious mind, now considered part of the brain stem. Albert Einstein even leveraged his unconscious mind (a dream) into his life's work.

> One workhorse of the digital mindset
> is the unconscious mind.
>
> Source: ingleyCONSULTANCY

How can you make your unconscious mind your workhorse? It would seem impossible to access a part of the mind that one is barely aware of. So, how do you do it?

You start by emptying your brain.

## Empty Your Brain

Emptying your brain is a way to tap into the unconscious mind.

If you systematically research and categorize information, the unconscious mind takes over quite easily if you empty your brain. That is, you walk away from your work and truly leave it behind. If you are at the very beginning of a project, this works best if you have already sliced out your big-picture issue and developed a long list of questions or an outline. The unconscious mind will move in and begin to work as a silent partner.

---

"Empty" your brain of all work and concerns to get your unconscious mind to work offline as a silent partner.

Source: ingleyCONSULTANCY

---

Surprisingly, it can be work to have an empty mind.

At times you will need to shift gears from intense research and organization to allowing and sometimes almost forcing your mind to be empty.

Allowing oneself the indulgence of an empty mind goes against the American ethic of hard work. Companies that do not think with the digital mindset have not caught on to the idea that an empty mind is busily solving problems in the background.

There is another aspect to this process. Emptying your brain means that unresolved emotional issues and perhaps even fear may surface.

## Resolving Unresolved Emotional Issues

You may realize at some point that unresolved emotional issues are making some of these changes more difficult. Actually, some emotional issues may always remain unresolved, but if you can put them away as you do a book on a shelf, you can be free of them. If you are currently confronting them and working through them, the power of the past can be minimized somewhat by this process of direct confrontation.

One tool from the right side of the brain is intuition. Strangely, intuition works both through the mind and through the body. In his book *Reinventing the Body, Resurrecting the Soul,* physician and spiritual leader Deepak Chopra advises, "If there's a conflict between your mind and body, trust your body." Trust your body to lead you to heal the past. My experience indicates that he is right, but one does have to wonder why!

"It's hard to let go of the past, but the magic is allowing yourself to replace it with something in the now," says author Laura Day in *How to Rule the World from Your Couch.*

With all the new information out there, there is plenty to replace whatever you are dealing with from the past

Part of rewiring your brain, then, is replacement.

There are also other ways to free oneself from the past. Much of one's suffering can come from getting results that one did not anticipate. For example, you complete a project thinking you will get accolades and it goes over like a lead balloon.

One of the best books I've read about living free from the past is *The Inner Game of Tennis.* Much of the book focuses on how to stay in the here and now, but tennis player and author Timothy Galwey also talks about the distinction between wanting to win and being attached to winning. You suffer when you are attached to winning and you do not get the results you wanted. You may also be attached to winning because of events from your past.

When you want to win or achieve a goal but you give up an attachment to it, you have that extra energy to use toward winning or achieving the goal. However, if you are attached to winning, it is like a pit bull with a bone in its mouth. You are using vital energy to try to control the results of what you do or how you are playing.

Other healing books you may wish to read are *How to Stop Worrying and Start Living* by Dale Carnegie, *The Power of Positive Thinking* by Norman Vincent Peale, and *Life Strategies* by Dr. Phil McGraw.

I have found that there can be much anguish in one's life from the "did me wrong" syndrome. There are three categories to this "did me wrong" syndrome: he did me wrong, she did me wrong and they did me wrong. "They" can be your boss, your company, your circumstances, or fill in the blank as appropriate. If you were to write down "They did me wrong" 500 times, you might find around the 399th time (assuming you got that far) that maybe you played a role. Psychiatrist David F. Allen, M.D., in his book *In Search of the Heart,* states that everyone has an "authority card," a concept he has developed and coined. The card gives you four inalienable rights: meaning, dignity, identity, and value. He goes on to say, "Some people go around collecting other people's authority cards and using them as credit cards to run up personal pleasures at someone else's expense." Setting boundaries is an important part of life and it is necessary to remember to play your card when appropriate in order to maintain meaning, dignity, identity, and value in your life.

Norman Vincent Peale's observation for handling events or circumstances that are tough is quite simple: Every knock is a boost.

## The Chatterbox

There is something we all have, and it is what has been called the chatterbox. This chatterbox really comes to life when you are trying something new, when you are frustrated, when things aren't going your way, or at other difficult times of your life. Generally speaking, the chatterbox is active at your most vulnerable moments. This chatterbox, emanating from some part of the brain that has yet to be pinpointed, is generally negative. It will tell you that you might not be quite up to the task. It will query about how you think you can do this. It will say that you are not good enough. The chatterbox exploits two common fears we all have: I'm not good enough, and I'm not lovable.

Ignoring the chatterbox is key to the digital mindset. You will never be able to empty your brain if you allow your chatterbox to chat away. Ignoring it is most of the battle. The replacement strategy already mentioned can also be implemented. The chatterbox has also been called the monkey mind, because it monkeys with your mind.

Quite a bit of territory has been covered here: the right and left sides of the brain, the role of the brain stem, emptying the brain, and having emotional issues arise from that emptying process. Clearly, all parts of the brain are needed for the digital mindset.

## Boosting the Power of Your Brain

There are some fairly simple ways to boost the power of your brain, priming it, if you will, for the deluge of change occurring over the next decade.

Exercise and diet count! Many say that fish is brain food. Whether you believe that or not, eating a nourishing diet low in chemical additives affects how you think. Experiment with foods to find the kind that is both delicious and good for you. There is something about the combination of tasty and nutritious that works.

Excitement in your life counts, too. Maybe it doesn't seem like the best moment of your life right now. Maybe you are having personal problems. Perhaps the world economic picture or the political situation is affecting you. It helps to make every day special in some way.

And repetition is very important. Repeatedly going over concepts, instructions, and methodologies is a way to make learning much easier. David Allen tries to impart this major lesson in his book *Getting Things Done*. Take a day a week, he says, and review everything. Yes, that's everything! Review your paper files, review your computer files. Know what is in every drawer, nook, and cranny. During this day of review, focus on review only. Yes, even go back and read those instruction manuals. It is a powerful way to learn, and it cannot be overestimated.

## Music and the Brain

In a way no one really understands, music has a profound effect on the brain. Physician and author Oliver Sacks published a book on the subject called *Musicophilia*. He describes how, with music, people with Parkinson's disease can move when otherwise they could not. Similar results happen when music is played to stroke victims, who begin to use words when before they could not speak.

I personally used music to tap into my own creativity. When I was just starting to write fiction and had insecurities about my ability to write, listening to *Chariots of Fire* inspired me and stirred creative juices. Today, it is impossible to listen to songs from that CD without remembering the effect it has had on my life.

You may wish to experiment with music as one mechanism to boost the power of your brain.

## Back to the Whole Brain

You likely have a better understanding of how your brain works and the importance of using it as completely as possible to leverage infinity.

For the book *Best of the Brain from Scientific American* edited by Floyd E. Bloom, M.D., Oliver Sacks provided a review statement for the jacket:

*The past two decades have brought amazing break-throughs in our understanding of the human brain, and our best scientist-writers have chronicled these quantum leaps in* Scientific American. *Now that we have these essays brought together and juxtaposed with one another in a single volume, we can suddenly see all of these connections and relationships—it is like seeing a great jigsaw puzzle, a whole intellectual landscape, taking shape.*

To Sacks, reading a wide variety of articles written about the brain is like seeing a great jigsaw puzzle taking shape. In a way, the digital mindset is just like that, but on a grander scale.

Viewing the world through the lens of the digital mindset is like seeing a giant jigsaw puzzle take shape. You will need to use your whole brain to view the world this way and put together your own giant jigsaw puzzle which is your life with the digital mindset. It is your own constellation of big pictures.

---

Viewing the world through the lens of the digital mindset is like seeing a giant jigsaw puzzle take shape.

Source: ingleyCONSULTANCY

---

## Making the Shift to Rewiring Your Brain to the Digital Mindset

Making the shift to rewiring your brain requires a decision to use not only the left and right sides of your brain but the unconscious part as well.

It is no longer enough to be just a logical, rational thinker. And it is not enough to be just an intuitive, holistic, and creative thinker. The digital mindset requires both.

And, because there is so much information out there and because sometimes it is difficult to see connections, the unconscious mind becomes more and more important.

Here are some questions to ask yourself.

1. What did I learn about myself from taking the spinning lady exercise?

   *My answer:* As already mentioned, I saw the lady spinning clockwise. I learned that it was uncomfortable for me to try to see it another way.

2. Do I see myself as left-brain dominant, or right-brain dominant or do I use both sides of my brain?

   *My answer:* Because I am left handed, I had always thought that I was right-brain dominant, and the test confirmed it. Much of what I do now seems to reflect that. I always knew that I tended to look at the "whole picture" but I did not really see myself as particularly creative, another characteristic of being right-brain dominant, until later in life. Because I've known I wasn't left-brain dominant, I have made a concerted effort to develop logical and rational skills, including getting an MBA and working in corporate finance. However, there are contradictions. I am a right-handed golfer but a left-handed tennis player.

# Take on the Digital Mindset Toolbox

To leverage infinity, a core concept of the digital mindset, you not only need to use your whole brain. You also must take on the digital mindset toolbox and use the tools there effectively.

The digital mindset toolbox organizes digital tools into categories that are easily understandable and do not necessitate—from an overview perspective—understanding all the features and functionalities of those tools.

The digital mindset toolbox contains five major tools: hardware, software, services, content, and accessories.

Hardware is the "black box" that allows the rest of the tools to function. Hardware doesn't work without software. Services (in conjunction with hardware and software) allow you access to content. Digital content and software (along with hardware) allow you to mix and match content in infinite ways. And it is through hardware, software, and services that you have access to digital storage for all of your digital content. Digital storage is really just hardware and software designed to store digital content. Digital content stored online has a fancier name: the cloud. Accessories give added benefit to the hardware, software, services, and content.

Continuing from a broad perspective, the infinite amount of information that we are trying to leverage with the digital mindset toolbox can be organized, as discussed in Step 1, into the triple play: audio/video (primarily digital TV), data (primarily broadband Internet), and voice (primarily phone).

Because hardware tools are only recently beginning to embrace the triple play, we are in a state of evolution and flux. Digital TV is still really audio/video in content and is just now moving into broadband Internet capabilities. Smart phones are best with data (primarily e-mail and text) and voice but are now starting to evolve with audio/video in a limited way and with more Web capabilities. PCs are currently the best at accommodating all three categories.

Because of this flux, we must put together a digital mindset toolbox that is not perfect but that can evolve as the marketplace gets more sophisticated and becomes better at accommodating infinity.

It is a patchwork quilt of sorts.

As you begin to see the digital mindset toolbox organized into these five categories, note that it isn't necessary at the outset to know everything about each category. It is important, however, to know the trends for each category. The trends will lead you to know better how deeply you wish to explore each category of tools.

Let's start with hardware tools: what they are and how they may evolve. Here we are using techniques of the digital mindset discussed later in the book in Steps 7 and 9.

## Hardware

Without hardware, there would be no software, services, access to content, or the ability to create digital content.

After all, what is a wireless service without a smart phone or other wireless device? What is a digital TV service without a digital TV or other device to receive the digital TV signal?

A first step to examining the hardware of the digital age is to look at its major components.

Hardware's current major categories—also known as the three screens—are digital TVs, PCs (Windows or Mac) and smart phones. Printers, e-book readers, tablets, MP3 players, digital cameras, digital camcorders, digital game consoles, and digital musical instruments are also categories of digital hardware but are not the heavy hitters of digital TVs, PCs, and smart phones.

Take note that new heavy hitters may be evolving. For example, from the above, a new heavy-hitter hardware category seems to be emerging: content accessing hardware that is connected to the Internet. This would be e-book readers, tablets, MP3 players and game consoles.

Where will digital hardware be in five, ten or fifteen years? The best guess is that, wherever possible, all major categories of digital hardware will accommodate audio/video, data, and voice via a broadband Internet service connection. In addition, hardware components will be more easily networked or connected together.

What is the most important hardware tool? Bill Gates once said, "I think it's fair to say that personal computers have become the most empowering tool we've ever created. They're tools of communication, they're tools of creativity, and they can be shaped by their user."

Gates does come from a somewhat biased perspective, but he may be right for now.

One category to watch is digital TV, which will be going through many changes over the next five to ten years.

Digital TV in the United States has just been liberated from analog waves because of the digital switch that took place in 2009. Those digital signals now coming into the home are 1s and 0s, and they can be mixed and matched.

This recently unchained industry—which has been limited for over seventy years by analog waves—is gearing up behind the scenes to make your digital TV much more like a PC, while trying to maintain the entertainment factor that allows TVs to remain distinct from a PC. There will be waves of changes to the TV over the next decade or so.

This wave of change is already beginning for the traditional TV set. In 2010, about 20% of the digital TVs sold in the United States will be able to connect to the Internet.

In the hardware category, watch also for devices that control the home, primarily the remote control. Note there is a behind-the-scenes battle between smart phones and universal remote control devices to become the major control device for the digital home. The remote control is currently the winner, but this may change over time.

## Software

Software's major categories are operating systems, word processing software, spreadsheets, presentation software, multimedia software, photography software, audio/video software, video software, audio software, and gaming software.

In most instances, you, the digital consumer, purchase either a hard copy (in general, a CD or DVD) or a download of the software.

The future of software, many say, is in the cloud. So, in lieu of having software in hard copy, it resides on a server at some distant location and is downloaded when needed. You never have to be concerned with upgrades because the software in the cloud is continuously being upgraded.

At some future point, the operating system for your PC might not be stored on your PC. Your PC would simply be a hardware device. You would turn it on and download the operating system. The same would be true for mobile phones and digital TVs.

Software can also be seen as a tool to create content. For example, Adobe Photoshop allows you to download photos and redesign them.

There is a fine line between software and content but it is useful to keep that distinction.

## Services

Services consist of the triple play which is audio/video, data and voice services or, said another way, digital TV, broadband Internet and phone. Adding wireless makes this the quadruple play, according to industry lingo. Wireless is actually a triple play of its own, because wireless phones or smart phones have evolved from primarily a phone service to phone, broadband Internet and digital TV services. It gets a bit confusing using terms that have evolved.

Cable TV service now includes broadband Internet and phone offerings, as well as its digital cable TV service. Satellite TV service has evolved in a similar fashion, offering broadband Internet and phone, as well as its satellite digital TV offering. In order to offer the triple play, satellite TV bundles technologies, because it cannot offer all three services over satellite the way cable TV can offer all three services via its cable into the home. Over-the-air digital TV service will evolve toward the triple play but is still primarily just audio/video. Broadband Internet service offers all three parts of the triple play: audio/video, data, and voice.

Landline voice is just that: phone service, although in some instances, it is bundled with broadband Internet.

Ultimately, it is about all three parts of the triple play: audio/video, data, and voice services. All categories of services will evolve toward the triple play. Therefore, it is useful to look at the future of each component of the triple play.

The future of audio/video transmission involves the ability to transmit the two major components of audio/video: movies and TV programs. Personal videos such as those seen on YouTube and the use of audio/video as part of other categories (for example, video resumes) are also important. The future of services for movies and TV programs involves availability for transmission (still in evolution for the smart phone, for example) and download time. The availability is heading toward ubiquity across hardware with Internet access and instantaneous download times.

The primary audio service as a subset of audio/video is radio. Radio is a fragmented industry in that it consists of many local stations and so it has been slow to change. Look for the pace to increase as more and more stations transmit with a digital signal.

The future of data services is aligned with the Internet and the future of the Internet. Much of the future of the Internet is information about information, that is, the ability to find the kind of information you are looking for in an easier fashion. Part of finding information will involve tagging. A tag (also known as metadata) is a key word or term assigned to a piece of information, be it audio/video, data or voice.

The future of voice services is the ability to use voice in a variety of new ways, including accessing voice mail in different ways and the ability to incorporate voice into different content. The use of voice in these new ways is already happening. Google has a service called Google Voice that, according to the company, "gives you one number for all phones, voicemail as easy as e-mail, free U.S. long distance, and low rates on international calls." The service allows you to choose a U.S. phone number. Any incoming calls to you are forwarded to whichever phone numbers you choose. For outgoing calls, you can dial using your Google Voice phone number.

## Content

Major categories of content are: Internet content, audio/video clips, video clips, audio clips, movies, TV programs, radio programs, books, photography, games, news media such as newspapers and magazines, and music.

All these areas are going through major changes and upheavals. Some areas, such as music, have already gone through major changes but more change is on the way.

You have probably noticed one trend in Internet content: You are participating in your online world in a more visible fashion than even five years ago. There are social media sites such as Facebook, Twitter, MySpace, and YouTube. There is blogging. There may be your own personal Web site. A family member may have created a genealogy site. You are now as much the content as mainstream content, and you can, with the right mix of marketing and savvy, become well known in a nontraditional way.

---

With the digital mindset, you are the content.

Source: ingleyCONSULTANCY

---

The future of audio/video content is tied into TV and the diverse devices that can receive TV, such as digital TVs, PCs, and smart phones.

YouTube is but one example of the future of video and how quickly one site can affect or influence the world. YouTube, it should be noted, is good example of you being the content.

Much of what is holding back video is the ability to find video clips. As information about video information becomes available, the video market is likely to grow exponentially.

The future of audio is also tied into the devices that receive it. A major part of audio is radio, which now can be received by satellite radios, HD radios, Internet radio, mobile phones, MP3 downloads, and pay TV audio channels. Audio is broadcast, streamed, downloaded, and podcast but faces the same issue video clips face: finding the clips. Note that all smart phones can have FM tuners and thus can become radios, which may change radio dramatically.

The future of movies, some would say, is tied up with 3D. In the past, 3D has had a difficult time launching and it is still unclear whether the upgrade to 3D for TVs will ever take off. Although not having to wear glasses for 3D viewing is forecasted for the future, for now you would have to wear glasses in the home. Most important is the cost factor and whether Americans will see the benefit of spending more for digital TVs and upgrading more frequently as new features like 3D become available.

The future of TV programs is that they will become more and more available through many more devices. That is also true for radio programs.

The future of books is all about changing to e-book readers and books online. When asked if the physical book will remain, Amazon's Jeff Bezos said: "You know, we love to get lost in an author's world. That's not going to go away; that's going to thrive. But the physical book really has had a 500-year run. It's probably the most successful technology ever. It's hard to come up with things that have had a longer run. If Gutenberg were alive today, he would recognize the physical book and know how to operate it immediately. Given how much change there has been everywhere else, what's remarkable is how stable the book has been for so long. But no technology, not even one as elegant as the book, lasts forever."

Bezos believes that the printed book will eventually disappear. He also believes that the form of the novel will remain but that most books, such as textbooks, will be reinvented.

Similar to books are newspapers and magazines. Their future, too, is connected to electronic devices such as the iPad and Kindle.

The future of photography is tied up in the way one preserves personal memories. Digital photography is a game changer in the ability to use photos as content and create photo books, digital scrapbooks and other personal memorabilia. The future of video games involves the devices on which these games are played. The robust video game console market has been dominated by three different types of consoles: the Microsoft Xbox, the Sony PlayStation, and the Nintendo Wii. Already these consoles are more than gaming devices, with each having an Internet connection: Xbox Live, PlayStation Network, and the Nintendo Virtual Console, respectively. As video games evolve for the masses and are targeted less exclusively at males in general and younger males in particular and more at the population at large, the video gaming marketplace, with its tie-in to movies, becomes an area to be watched.

Music, given that it was the first type of specialized content to be widely successful on the Internet (at the expense of copyrights), has a tormented online past but still has a great digital future. The immense success of the iPod and iTunes is a harbinger of music's Internet future.

## Accessories

The proliferation of accessories for such devices as the iPod has been phenomenal. Walk through any high tech store and you will see an amazing array of accessories. Another category of accessories is the apps that have evolved for the iPhone. In a way, they can be seen as software accessories, but they can also be seen as a new category of content.

## Plug and Play

Eventually, there will be an easy "plug and play" among digital devices. For the moment, the marketplace is in transition toward true convergence when all digital hardware will interface with all other digital hardware as appropriate and all hardware can be connected to a network.

No matter where the technology is on the continuum, and even as it reaches true convergence, with the digital mindset, learning is a constant.

## A Constant Every Day

Every day is a potential day in which one's world can be turned upside down by a new product or service that is announced or by information that one learns. Constant learning is a necessity with the digital mindset.

---

With the digital mindset, learning is a constant.

Source: ingleyCONSULTANCY

---

In other words, you need to incorporate constant learning into your daily activities. Constant learning can consist of "bite-sized" moments and it is likely that learning in bite-sized pieces is an effective learning method. Repetition, as already discussed, is another effective learning method.

## Media Mogul

With the digital mindset, you have moved into a much more powerful place than you were. You are now essentially a media mogul and as such, you are in control of the equivalent of running a small business.

---

With the digital mindset, you become a media mogul, in control and more powerful than you have ever been.

Source: ingleyCONSULTANCY

---

However you view your new position as media mogul, the digital "home" (be it home, office, boat, car or wherever) is, in fact, the new homestead. You are renting services and leveraging hardware, software, content, and accessories, living and cultivating your tract by using the digital mindset.

---

The digital home is the new homestead. You cultivate the tract by using the digital mindset.

Source: ingleyCONSULTANCY

---

## Making the Shift to Taking on the Digital Mindset Toolbox

Classifying and categorizing the diverse array of digital choices is one way to get a handle on the enormous choices one has as a digital consumer.

Here are some questions to ask yourself.

1. What are the main components of my digital mindset toolbox?

   *My answer:* Everyone creates their own main components. If you are a photographer by trade, your digital mindset toolbox will be different from someone who is a graphics designer. The three main hardware devices of the digital mindset toolbox are a PC (Windows or Mac), smart phone, and digital TV. I try to stay focused on the three main devices.

2. How do I keep up with all of the changes to the digital mindset toolbox?

   *My answer:* To keep up with all the changes, I maintain folders both electronically and physically. You might create a file called Five Major Tools with subfolders for hardware, software, services, content, and accessories. Some Web sites such as HowardForums.com and BestBuy.com can help. You can also visit such sites as Microsoft.com and Apple.com.

# Make Organization a Top Priority

Organization emerges as a top priority when you take on the concepts of embracing and leveraging infinity.

The term organization is used here in the broadest sense: organization of your home, work space, projects, time, schedule, and relationships. Add in anything else you think applies.

Victor Hugo once said: "He who every morning plans the transactions of the day and follows out that plan, carries a thread that will guide him through the maze of the most busy life. But where no plan is laid, where the disposal of time is surrendered merely to the change of incidence, chaos will soon reign."

That was said more than a hundred years ago. Surely, life has changed.

Yes, it has. The digital world is more fast-paced and voluminous than the world of Hugo, yet the basic principle remains. Where you have no plan, chaos will soon reign.

The best plan to have is organization.

## Oil for the Digital Gears

Inherent in the digital age are swift changes. Hardware changes quickly. Software upgrades are constant. Services change as hardware and software get more sophisticated. Content is an always expanding resource. Accessories (for example, for the iPhone) can be rolled out in the hundreds.

It is a daunting task to even begin to keep up with all the changes, and that's just the digital mindset toolbox. It has nothing to do with what you may want to accomplish, such as write a family cookbook, research a disease, or find a vet for your pet.

With the digital mindset, you take on organization in a way that you never have. You have already accepted infinity. You have already accepted constant change.

Organization is oil for the digital gears, so to speak.

---

Organization is oil for the digital gears.

Source: ingleyCONSULTANCY

---

You might say that you work best in "disorganization," and that may be. . . *for now*. But in the digital age, when you might have more information coming to you in a day than you used to in a month, rejecting organization is no longer an option.

## An Uncluttered Mind

Beyond the sheer speed of change in the digital age, there is another, very important reason to get organized.

The digital mindset demands an uncluttered mind. Remember that you are dealing with infinity here. The universe of the digital age is so vast that were you to try and keep everything present in your mind, you would soon be so bogged down that you wouldn't want to even climb out of bed in the morning.

---

The digital mindset demands
an uncluttered mind.

Source: ingleyCONSULTANCY

---

The goal is to be able to walk down the street so carefree that you feel like whistling. Or, if you can whistle, you may soon be doing just that. Perhaps it's time for whistling to make a comeback.

There's another reason to get organized. That's because the digital mindset abhors inefficiency.

---

The digital mindset abhors inefficiency.

Source: ingleyCONSULTANCY

---

That's abhor, as in dislike intensely or loathe. There's just too much information out there to allow inefficiency to play a role.

There are now entire books on organization, TV shows dedicated to organizational techniques, and many articles written about the process.

Where does one begin? And what's the best system to use?

## To Get Help or Not to Get Help

You, like me, may have tried different systems. Perhaps you have engaged an organization consultant or professional organizer. I have.

I was once working with an organization consultant in the 1990s and explained that I was overwhelmed by the amount of mail I received. It was always piling up.

As she picked up a very large stack of mail, she said to me, "I can sort this for you in one minute." I took her challenge on and timed her with my watch's second hand. Sure enough, within one minute, she was able to go through the entire stack. As it turns out, most of it was junk mail or trade magazines and could be thrown out or put into a reading file.

Organization consultants can help you develop systems that work. These days, I seldom find I need one. For some, however, it might be the right time to hire such a consultant. It helps the process along, and that might be what is needed at this stage of your life.

For others, a lack of organization is a major issue in their lives. Although the condition of hoarding is at the extreme, many folks lose valuable time daily looking for items (including searching for items filed away online) or realizing that they are not stocked with the appropriate basic supplies. They may actually have these basic supplies but simply do not know where they are.

Whatever might have been holding you back, with the digital mindset, you will need to take organizing more seriously.

## Consistency Is Key

The main issue of organization is that it's not that hard. It doesn't take that long. You just have to *do it,* and, with the digital mindset, you have to *do it on a daily basis.*

You cannot possibly have an organization consultant with you at all times. So, the key is to become your own organization consultant.

Another compelling reason to do it yourself is that organizing is an ever-changing process. Systems will always have to be refined.

## What Type Are You?

I once read a list of the different categories of people and how they handle organization. My category, or at least the one I related to, was: "You get your fix on Route 66." You got it. I'd rather be out having fun. Okay, I've gotten better. I now try to organize first.

Since I don't remember the other categories, I have created my own from observing others. There are four types.

Type 1: Organized Inside and Outside

This organization type is *organized.* The drawers are organized, the closets are organized, the computer files are organized. Plus, the home is organized on the outside. Visually, it is a home that is a pleasure to look at and be in.

Type 2: Organized Outside but Not Inside

This organization type makes you believe that they are completely organized. Their home is beautiful. Everything is in its place. It's clean, neat and tidy wherever you look. However, open a drawer and you will see that it doesn't extend to the inside. A variation of this type has a basement or garage that collects everything.

Type 3: Organized Inside but Not Outside

Then there is the organization type who does have ordered closets, drawers, and files but where you may find disorder on the outside. That is, visually, the home may not be seen as neat and tidy, but there is more order than meets the eye.

Type 4: Disorganized Inside and Outside

This type is disorganized to the extreme. Everything is in disarray.

It doesn't really matter which type you are. What matters is that you take the task of organizing your life more seriously.

Let's say that you are now taking on organization for some aspect of your life.

Organization consultants often start with the principle "like with like."

## Like with Like

"Like with like" applies equally well for your digital assets as it does for your non-digital assets such as papers, clothing, kitchen equipment, and toiletries. There are two steps in the like-with-like process: sort like with like and organize like with like. Sorting is simply piling together like or similar items. Organizing is taking those like or similar items and putting them away in an easy-to-use fashion.

Once you have sorted "likes" into piles, you will notice that you may not want to keep all the items. Like piles emerge into three subpiles: discard, give away, or keep.

The discard and give away piles are self-explanatory. Note that you will need to do this weeding out process for both your digital assets and your non-digital assets.

It is the "keep" pile that takes up your time.

Let's start with a non-digital and easy example from the home, kitchen cupboards that are in disarray. Using this system, you begin by finding all of the glasses and put them in one area. Then you find all of the pots and pans and put those in a different area. Do the same with dishes and silverware. That's the high-level sort. The next step is to discard or give away items that you do not want.

The next sort of like with like is to find, for example, all dishes in one pattern. You then sort those dishes by dinner plates, salad bowls, saucers, cups and so on.

This system may appear obvious to you. In fact, you may be a super organizer. Wherever you are starting, this like with like can be applied to your digital assets as well.

The like-with-like sorting pattern is particularly useful for digital data files (your own information plus information gleaned from Web sites). Examples that can use this system include digital content such as songs, photos, videos, digital contact file, and your favorites file for storing frequently visited Web sites.

Let's say that you also keep a paper file system. Take three examples: personal financial records, genealogy, and school information.

Using Microsoft software, you would need to go into your computer files (My Documents in Windows) and create three folders: personal financial records, genealogy, and school information.

For synergy, you would go to your Web Favorites and create three folders: personal financial records, genealogy, and school information. You could also go into your Outlook e-mail inbox and create three folders: personal financial records, genealogy, and school information. You might also have Contacts folders for these three categories.

Finally, assuming you have a paper file system, you could create three hanging folders: personal financial records, genealogy, and school information.

This starts to get very powerful if you create subfolders as well across your systems and it is just one way to organize.

I have found that the simpler the approach and the more times the categories show up across systems, the easier it is to track everything in your life.

## Digital Assets

So far, the focus has been examining your life as a whole in terms of organizing. Let's shift the focus to just your digital assets in your home. These assets include all hardware, software, services, content, and accessories that you have as part of your digital home. The major change is that you must now see your digital assets as a cost center. Although this is an organization step, seeing your digital assets as a cost center alters their importance.

---

The digital mindset sees digital
assets as a cost center.

Source: ingleyCONSULTANCY

---

Most current financial gurus who write books and appear on TV have yet to mention this. My presumption is that they assume that digital assets are some sort of add-on to your life. They are not simply an add-on. With the digital mindset, your digital assets are as critical to your life as food, shelter, health care, clothes, and transportation.

You will need to organize your digital assets from the outside and from the inside.

It is extremely important that you weed out older digital hardware, software, services, content, and accessories—anything that is out of date or that you do not use. Because the digital mindset is all about efficiency, that efficiency must include your digital assets.

This experience could be a painful one if you have purchased expensive gadgets or expensive services that you do not use. If it is difficult to part with a component that was expensive but is not in use, chalk it up to the digital learning curve. When change is the norm, predicting what will be useful in the future is not always easy. There should be a certain percentage of your digital dollar that can be written off to good choices at the time but without a long-term benefit.

Begin by gathering all your digital assets (save for the largest components such as digital TVs) and put them in one place, such as a dining room table. You may be surprised to find old mobile phones and connectors that you have no idea where they came from.

Accessories such as cables and connectors are sometimes difficult to find when you need them. If you don't know what something is, throw it away. Get a stack of large ziplock bags and begin to put what you can identify inside a bag. Label the bag. Put all of these ziplock bags in one place such as a drawer or large basket or container. If you couldn't part with the unknown connectors, put them all together and label the bag "unknown."

Gather all paper instruction manuals and put them in one file section for easy reference. If these manuals are electronic, create an Instruction Manuals folder.

## Inboxes

You can think of anything coming in that has not been sorted as a giant inbox. Examples include e-mail, paper mail, groceries purchased, new clothes purchased and stuff that still needs to be sorted.

The easiest way to deal with everything incoming is sorting like with like.

Still, the issue of the e-mail inbox is one that gets many complaints. How do you manage it all?

A distinction made by a *Wall Street Journal* columnist is that there are two types of e-mail users: hoarders and deleters. One type keeps everything, the other processes everything.

With the digital mindset, you mix and match ideas. I think you can be both a hoarder and a deleter. You can devise a system whereby you copy everything that comes in (you will need a demarcation system here) to a file called Inbox Duplicate. You can do the same with your sent mail file. If the point of the digital age is to have easy access to information, it stands to reason that you can keep an extra copy of an e-mail just in case.

Then, with the knowledge that you have a duplicate, you can do what you wish with your inbox: delete or create folders to move mail into.

Alternatively, you may use the delete folder as a backup system. The delete folder will not have a complete record, however, of all the incoming mail, as some e-mails will have been filed by you into folders.

## Project Management Versus Time Management

Even if you are able to organize all your assets, you still may not find yourself organized.

Let's return to the big-picture concept. Big pictures that you have identified in your life can likely be broken down into projects. Getting a job can be a big-picture item in your life that can be broken into projects such as researching the global market, researching the local market, putting together a resume, and putting together a short list of companies you find interesting.

The key is to identify and manage projects in the digital age within the context of a big picture. Some of what you want to accomplish can just be seen as projects.

A project can be sorting your desk drawer or it can be planning a dinner party. Or it might be a summer vacation or a work assignment.

Everything you do in the digital age can be put on a project status. This should include your own well-being.

## Seeing Your Home as Centers

Another powerful way to look at your life is as centers. Whatever needs to be maintained can be seen as a center. There is a kitchen center, an entertainment center, a bathroom center, a digital asset center, a transportation center, a finance center, and a work center.

## A Complete System: 5S

If you are looking for a complete system, you might want to try one that was developed by the Japanese. It is called 5S. Each step begins with the letter S. These steps are:

Seiri (sort)

Seiton (set in order)

Seiso (shine)

Seiketsu (standardize)

Shitsuke (stick to it)

These steps are similar to what has already been discussed.

## Knowing Where Everything Is

The goal here is to know where everything is. But even the best-organized systems need revisiting.

Repetition is key. That is how the brain works best—through repetition.

Some live in chaos and claim to still know where everything is. It is possible that a system that is chaotic will continue to work as the digital age matures, but it is not probable. The fast-paced changes characteristic of this new age need to be managed in a new way. One of the best ways to cope with these fast-paced changes is to know where everything is via an organized environment.

It is thrilling to watch home makeover TV shows when someone walks into a room in complete disarray and, during the course of the show, completely transforms the room. What the shows do not say is whether these rooms actually stay that way.

You, too, can transform your home quickly. Keep in mind that the transformation is but a small part of the challenge. Maintenance is a process. This process is repetitive. Part of the process is relearning your system and the contents of that system once a week. Relearning means going back and seeing where everything is.

## Making the Shift to Making Organization a Top Priority

Making organization a top priority is easy for anyone for the short term. The challenge is maintaining the habits over the long term.

Here are some questions to ask yourself.

1. What aspect of organizing is easiest for me?

   *My answer:* I find it easiest to be organized from the inside out. Because I have experimented with different systems, the process is easier now than it has been in the past. Still, it is a constant journey and a constant challenge for me.

2. Is organization already a top priority for me?

   *My answer:* Around the mid-1990s, I began to make organization a top priority. It was partly because I was reading so many trade magazines that I needed a system to keep on top of all the articles that I thought important enough to be part of a file system. Looking for the secret ingredient to this process, I began to hire different organization consultants. In the back of my mind was the thought that they knew a whole lot more about all this than I did. Although on some level they did know more than I did, it slowly became clear that what I was searching for was never going to be provided. What I really wanted to understand was how to have the amount of time to read everything as well as have the time to create a file system for it all. After more than a decade of struggling with this, my best solution is to skim the article and file it so that I can find it later. I can always go back and read it more carefully. The process applies to both online articles and physical ones. This method works for me.

3. How can I make organization important over the long term?

   *My answer:* There is no easy answer to this question. Making a commitment to yourself is one step. The real power to organizing information is to change that organization method from time to time. That is what I do. You can reinterpret material in this way. This facility in reorganizing, however, only happens over the long haul.

# Layer Creativity into Your Life

A core concept of the digital mindset is creativity. To benefit fully from the digital mindset, you will need to layer creativity into your life.

## What Is Creativity?

Ernest Hemingway once said, "There is nothing to writing. All you do is sit down at a typewriter and bleed."

In a similar, albeit happier, vein, Pablo Picasso suggested, "If you paint, close your eyes and sing."

Yet it may be Albert Einstein who really hit the nail on the head when he said, "The secret to creativity is knowing how to hide your sources." Einstein is saying that creativity builds on pre-existing work. It is simply mixing and matching *existing* building blocks—such as bricks, words, paint and, yes, digits—in a new way.

A childhood friend, now a well-known artist, once told me that the key to unlocking his creativity was the phrase "iron butterfly." He didn't explain further, and for years I thought that perhaps he was referring to the music group Iron Butterfly and something in their music allowed his creativity to flow. Wrong! I have never confirmed it with him, but I am fairly certain now that the phrase "iron butterfly" signified to him the mixing and matching that is inherent in any creative act, and it is the mixing and matching of concepts and characteristics that are not usually found together. Iron is hard, cold, inflexible, and not colorful; butterflies are delicate, light, and colorful.

Mixing and matching elements, characteristics, and concepts that are not generally associated with one another is what creativity really is.

---

The mixing and matching of elements,
characteristics, and concepts that are
not generally associated with one another
is at the heart of creativity.

Source: ingleyCONSULTANCY

---

Communications theorist Marshall McLuhan coined the phrase "The medium is the message" and used it as a first chapter in his book *Understanding Media*. Later, he named a book *The Medium Is the Massage*, playing with his own coined phrase.

The phrase can be mixed and matched in any number of ways. Note how the mixing and matching creates new phrases with different meanings.

The medium is the message.

The medium is the massage.

The medium is tedium.

The tedium is the message.

The tedium is medium.

The message is medium.

The massage is medium.

The massage is tedium.

The massage is the message.

## A Mix-and-Match Example of Creativity

A "book" entitled *The Official Movie Plot Generator* by brothers Jason and Justin Heimberg, both screenwriters in Los Angeles, demonstrates the mix-and-match thinking behind creativity. They have taken 90 index-style cards and put them into three piles of 30 cards each. These three piles are then spiral-bound together. By flipping through the book, you can create 27,000 movie plot combinations. That's 30 times 30 times 30 or 27,000. This type of recombination is a good demonstration of what creativity really is.

## A New Category of Creativity

Creativity that gets attention has beauty or meaning attached to it in some way. It enlightens you. Art is creativity in its highest form

Creativity has traditionally been associated with music, art, acting, writing, photography, building, and architecture

With the digital mindset, the definition of creativity expands. In the digital world, creativity is all about mixing and matching 1s and 0s.

With the digital mindset, creativity is simply another tool added to the traditional brick-and-mortar tools of bricks, words, paint and other types of building instruments. The digital mindset sees that a whole new category exists—digits—and that these digits can be creatively mixed and matched.

---

The digital mindset increases
the creative landscape by adding the
mixing and matching of digits to more
traditional forms of creativity.

Source: ingleyCONSULTANCY

---

## Database as a Foundation

Increasing your own database increases the possibilities for creativity because you have more raw materials at your fingertips. The type of database that you develop will vary according to what you are focusing on. It may be a file system using file cabinets or computer files to assemble articles, or it might be assembling other kinds of materials such as photographs or videos.

Again, creativity in the digital mindset is all about mixing and matching digits in new ways.

## Creative Space

Creativity cannot occur if all your time is booked. Remember that one of the tools to be leveraged is the unconscious mind. Creativity requires creative space. You have to have the downtime for creativity.

Take Google, for example. Google allows its employees to commit 80% of their time. That gives them 20% downtime or time to think about their own projects.

The results? Google is one of the most successful companies in the world.

Most companies do not value the creative space, but that will likely change as more and more companies take on the digital mindset.

## The Golden Hours

You may find that you have what I call golden hours. These are the hours in the day when you are the most creative.

I am the most creative from 5 a.m. until 9 a.m. Yet, now I find that I can experiment with those hours and sometimes shift them.

Find your golden hours and leverage them. Play around with them.

There is power in finding the hours when you are at your best.

## Observing Structure

You cannot be creative if you have not observed and understood structure. Creativity requires understanding structure.

How is a book constructed? How is a painting made? How is a song's music composed? How are the song's lyrics put together?

Become aware of how products and services are designed. How is your digital TV designed? What kind of connections does it have? How is your PC designed? What kind of connections does it have?

What in the design is not "user friendly"? What would you do differently if you were to design it?

Structure is key because creativity is about rearranging structure.

## Creative Process

The process of being creative is the process of moving from something that is unremarkable work to something that is high-quality work. It is the willingness to push forward that makes all the difference. Another word for this process is persistence.

In other words, you have to be willing to be really bad at something before you are able to be good at it. When I begin a book, the initial version has more to do with ideas than actual writing. I try to get as many ideas down as possible. Someone might look at this early draft and say, "A sixth grader can write better than this." That may be true. But, at that moment, my mind is only focused on ideas and not words. The polishing of the words comes later.

---

With the digital mindset, you accept the process of moving from imperfection and rough ideas to high-quality work.

Source: ingleyCONSULTANCY

---

## Creating Your Own Magic Formula

With the digital mindset, you can create your own magic formula.

---

With the digital mindset, you can create your own magic formula.

Source: ingleyCONSULTANCY

---

Magic formulas can be seen as private strategies. You do not want to share your magic formula. Then, it's no longer magic! Once your magic formula becomes public, it really becomes a stated strategy.

To get an idea what a magic formula is, here are two from a Web search.

An article "Creating a Magic Formula" on Google Finance revealed the following:

> *Here's a little secret. I spend most of my online time on a handful of sites. In particular, I spend about 80% of my time on two sites. The first is Morning-star.com in which I am a premium user and use it mostly to do basic security analysis, look at 10 years of financial data, etc. Secondly, I spend a ton of time on Google Finance.*

Note that this really is no longer a magic formula but rather now a stated strategy.

Another magic formula was revealed by Bonnie Hammer, president of NBC Universal Cable Entertainment. She said that her team had developed "a filter for the station's content that aimed to create smart, fun escapism." Of course, the details of that filter would be corporate confidential, so it is still magic. As soon as the details of the filter are made public, this magic filter formula becomes a stated strategy.

Suppose you are a graphics designer but in your spare time like to paint in water colors. You would really like to have these two parts of your life connected. You might create a magic formula whereby both of these talents come together professionally and personally. It doesn't need to be a well-formulated statement.

It's a magic formula if it stays private. Maybe you prefer to state your strategies. That works, too. Finding a magic formula for yourself is, well, magical!

## Creativity Synonymous with Opportunity

Another exciting aspect of the digital mindset is that creativity becomes synonymous with opportunity.

---

With the digital mindset, creativity becomes synonymous with opportunity.

Source: ingleyCONSULTANCY

---

Creativity requires that you view things in a new way. Viewing things in a new way ultimately leads to opportunity. When you look at things in these new ways, you will see alternative ways to solve problems or will recognize ideas that will be helpful to others.

The key is to bring a new perspective to the table, and that's what the digital mindset gives you: a new perspective.

How might this play out?

Here are some possible steps.

Step 1. Start with defining your big picture, project, or problem.

Step 2. Search and read as much as you can about the problem itself and about the key words that you associate with the problem. Put this information all in one folder with subfolders using the key words. As you search on the Internet, be on the lookout for books that may have solutions. Create a folder name that says Books or create a subfolder for books.

Step 3. After your search ends, go back and read everything.

Step 4. Create subfolders for the topics that recur.

Step 5. Create an outline if you are writing something.

Step 6. Flesh out the outline.

Step 7. Reflect.

Step 8. Digest.

Step 9. Go back to see if you can find an innovative way to mix and match the data to improve the current structure.

Step 10. Create by writing, programming, drawing, designing, or whatever is the focus of your big picture, project or problem.

## Creativity and Companies of the Information Age

How have companies taken on the digital mindset? More to the point, *have* companies taken on the digital mindset?

Let's take a look. Keep in mind the building blocks of the digital mindset: hardware, software, services, content, and accessories.

Apple presents a good example. Steve Jobs left Apple involuntarily in 1985 after having created a hardware and software company. Later, he became involved with Pixar and began getting an education in digitized content: how to take hand-drawn techniques and apply them to computers to produce animation.

Having in-depth knowledge of these three "tools" in his toolbox—hardware, software, and content—proved powerful when he returned to Apple a decade later. It should come as no surprise that his "mixing and matching" of hardware ideas, software ideas, and content ideas would result in the iPod, a clever combination of—yes—hardware, software, and content. iTunes, of course, is part of that "content" rearrangement or creative take on how to sell songs on the Internet.

It should be predictable, then, that Jobs would want to move into services, making his creative palette now hardware, software, content, and services.

Hence, Apple came out with the iPhone. But wait. The iPhone became even more interesting with iPhone apps. Now, Jobs is playing with hardware, software, content, services, and accessories (apps can be seen as both software and accessories to the iPhone). The iPad has followed the success of the iPhone and, like the iPhone, employs all five of the tool categories from the digital mindset toolbox. The evolution of these products and services from Apple shows creative mixing and matching of the elements of the digital mindset toolbox.

It wouldn't be terribly fair to look at Apple without also mentioning Microsoft. Microsoft developed an operating system known as MS-DOS. The original IBM PC gave the consumer a choice of three operating systems, one of which was MS-DOS. Because Microsoft had licensed the system to IBM at a low price, IBM offered MS-DOS to consumers at a lower price than the other operating systems. Microsoft saw this as inexpensive marketing, theorizing that only one operating system would ultimately succeed with the IBM PC. In addition, Microsoft guessed that as the popularity of MS-DOS grew through IBM PC sales, it could license the MS-DOS system to other PC manufacturers. Of course, the rest is history, as IBM ultimately chose to use the least expensive operating system and Microsoft was able to license MS-DOS to other PC manufacturers.

What is important here is the creative out-of-the-box thinking in business strategy by Microsoft. Microsoft currently makes most of its money from Microsoft Office (part of its Business Division), followed by Windows Operating System (part of its Client Division) and then XBox (a key component of its Entertainment and Devices Division). It is able to stay powerful by continuing the out-of-the-box business strategy it formulated with MS-DOS and using it with Microsoft Office and Windows Operating System. One can see, however, that with cloud computing and the coming ability to download software on an "as needed" basis there is a vulnerability here. Another out-of-the-box creative business strategy will need to be formulated for dealing with the cloud. Innovation and creativity must be ever evolving, no matter what company you are.

## Creating Your Own Job and Job Opportunities

With the digital mindset, you create your own job and job opportunities.

You start with asking the right questions. Is there growth potential in the United States—or, if you don't live in the United States, your country—for what you want to do?

---

With the digital mindset, you create your own job and job opportunities.

Source: ingleyCONSULTANCY

---

Is this job in danger of being exported? Is it becoming superfluous?

What can you do on your own to create a unique "package" that employers will want to have?

Are you an entrepreneur? We all are, in our own way, but the question you need to ask, Is this an employment avenue you wish to take? Many do not want to go this route, even if they have the skills. You need to know this about yourself.

Creating the mental picture helps that job happen.

A 2007 article in the *Wall Street Journal* was entitled "Recipe for Creating New Products: Take Two Completely Separate Categories—Combine." The theme of the article by Michael Gibbert and David Mazursky is that instead of always thinking of improving your brand by increments, think instead of "cross-branding" them.

For example, a shoe and the iPod have been combined by Nike and Apple. The shoe has a special pocket under the insole for a sensor that connects to a person's iPod. The sensor tracks a person's run, for example, and sends the data to the iPod.

Just out of thin air, here are two completely different concepts that I've grabbed: genealogy and my living room couch. One could start a Web site called the Couch Potato Genealogy Club. Not so dissimilar after all. One could create a word Couchealogy—exploring genealogy from the homefront. That is the heart of creativity: take two seemingly unrelated concepts and put them together in a unique fashion that gives them power. Creativity, then, is all about the "iron butterfly."

With the digital mindset, you can mix and match your talents as well, therein creating your own brand. It is certainly a good technique for finding a job that your cross-brand ideally fills.

---

With the digital mindset, you are your own brand.

Source: ingleyCONSULTANCY

---

## McLuhan and the New Message

Today, Marshall McLuhan can be reinterpreted.

In 1964, Marshall McLuhan wrote in the first chapter of *Understanding Media* entitled "The Medium is the Message": "For the 'message' of any medium or technology is the change of scale or pace or pattern that it introduces into human affairs."

The message of digital technology is that the change of scale or pace or pattern that it introduces into your life is exponentially large. Like an octopus reaching out in all directions, it affects virtually everything.

But you can view what McLuhan was saying in a slightly different, more out-of-the-box way. That is, instead of viewing the message of digital technology as the huge change it introduces into our affairs largely from content put together by large companies, you are now more directly the message. With YouTube, Facebook, LinkedIn, MySpace, Twitter, and a whole slew of other social networking sites, you as the message has implications that no one fully understands yet. You as the message is a major shift in communication. Your own creativity can be experienced by a broad audience with a simple download of photos, videos, text, voice or any combination of content.

---

With the digital mindset, you are the message.

Source: ingleyCONSULTANCY

---

It is fascinating to look back at another book by McLuhan (coauthored with Quentin Fiore), first published in 1967.

Called *The Medium is the Massage*, the book might more appropriately be entitled *The Medium Has Been Massaged*, as it is a book of collages. McLuhan and Fiore state on page 3 of the book:

> *Our time [1967] is for crossing barriers, for erasing old categories—for probing around. When two seemingly disparate elements are imaginatively poised, put in opposition in new and unique ways, startling discoveries often result.*

This quote is a memorable definition of creativity, and the book itself demonstrates the quote. McLuhan was ahead of his time and would be in his element today.

## Making the Shift to Layering Creativity into Your life

Creativity fits right into the digital mindset. That's because it is all about mixing and matching, a core digital mindset concept.

Here are some questions to ask yourself about layering creativity into your life.

1. Is creativity currently an active part of your life?

   *My answer:* Creativity is an active and important part of my life. Until around 1990, I did not, however, see myself as particularly creative.

The turning point was working at MCI. Bill McGowan, the CEO of the company, encouraged creative and innovative thinking. It was the only way to compete effectively against the much larger AT&T. I wish McGowan were still alive; he had a vision for what is happening now back in the 1980s. I am indebted to him for creating a business atmosphere that supported out-of-the box thinking.

2. How do you plan to layer creativity into your life in the near future?

*My answer:* I plan to layer creativity into my life in the near future in every way possible. This might sound like I'm not answering the question, so I'll try and be more specific. My plan is to add creative touches to my cooking, more books are in the works plus I am writing lyrics to songs. My goal is to do everything with a mix-and-match approach.

# Employ Digital Workhorses

Lucille Ball once—perhaps not so famously—said, "The more you learn, the more you can learn."

Never is that more obvious than with the digital mindset.

---

With the digital mindset, the more you learn, the more you can learn.

Source: ingleyCONSULTANCY

---

But how can you really do that? How is it that, with more and more information coming your way every day, you really *can* learn more?

One way to learn more is to employ digital workhorses. One workhorse (albeit not digital) has already been discussed: your unconscious mind. The major digital workhorses are search engines, data exhaust, alerts, social media, synchronization across devices, devices communicating with one another, customized home pages, "Web employees," and data hubs. These digital workhorses sort through data, categorize data, keep one informed, perform duties, and save time.

To get the most from digital workhorses, more information about the finite world of data would be useful. Let's shift the focus from the infinite data possibilities through mixing and matching to the finite data world that is currently online.

## Finite Data

The amount of data "out there" is daunting and can be seen in terms of bytes as follows:

| Data Unit | Bytes | Size |
| --- | ---: | ---: |
| Bit | 0 | 1 or 0 |
| Byte | 1.00 | One byte can create 1 English letter |
| Kilobyte | 1,024.00 | One page of typed text is 2 KB |
| Megabyte | 1,048,576.00 | One song about 4 MB |
| Gigabyte | 1,073,741,824.00 | 2 hour film compressed to 1–2 GB |
| Terabyte | 1,099,511,627,776.00 | Library of Congress catalog about 15 TB |
| Petabyte | 1,125,899,906,842,620.00 | Google processes about 1 PB of data every hour |
| Exabyte | 1,152,921,504,606,850,000.00 | 10 billion copies of the Economist |
| Zettabyte | 1,180,591,620,717,410,000,000.00 | Total amount of existing information about 1.2 ZB |
| Yottabyte | 1,208,925,819,614,630,000,000,000.00 | Big! |

Source: Economist

From purely a "byte" perspective, one byte can be used to create one letter in the English alphabet. One kilobyte (KB) is equivalent to about one-half page of typed text. Note that 1 KB of data is not precisely 1,000 bytes but rather 1,024 bytes. Be that as it may, conventional notation often says 1,000 bytes.

One megabyte is about 1 million bytes. One gigabyte is about 1 billion bytes and 1 terabyte is about 1 trillion bytes. As the size of data gets larger, the generic name for that amount is more remote. As it turns out, the next term in the series after trillion is quadrillion, and that's what a petrabyte is: 1 quadrillion bytes. That's the amount of data that Google processes every hour according to the *Economist.*

The total amount of information that now exists is about 1.2 zettabytes or 1.2 sextillion bytes of data.

This information now has a new name: "big data." Big data—and getting bigger all the time—can be managed with digital workhorses.

## Big Data, Search Engines and You

You undoubtedly already employ one digital workhorse to handle "big data": the search engine.

Search engines were created based on software called algorithms. Algorithms solve problems. In the case of search, an algorithm is used to consider more than 500 million variables and 2 billion terms. According to this algorithm, pages are ranked, with the one at the top of the list considered the most important.

Already discussed is the idea of creating a big picture based on an issue or problem that you are trying to solve. Creating a list of questions has also been discussed. These questions can be viewed as packets or algorithms. If you get really smart at putting together your own algorithm, you may be able to mine some important data from online sources.

With the digital mindset, thinking like a search engine is a necessity.

---

With the digital mindset, thinking like a search engine is a necessity.

Source: ingleyCONSULTANCY

---

Soon, after you have plugged in your series of question to a search engine, you will have a thread to follow. And, following the thread means that you may not end up where you thought you would once you complete a search.

Skillful searchers find unusual connections or hidden tidbits of information and follow those tidbits as well. It is an intuitive, right-brain activity.

## Search Engines: Information about Information

One can see knowledge on four levels. Knowledge is content digested, understood and analyzed. Knowledge is also knowing where to look to find answers and information.

For this reason, the area of search is almost holy in the way it is revered. Google, as the premier search engine company, is seen as more than just a company.

Search gives you information about information. And information about information, if it is good information about information, allows you to increase your knowledge base with a minimum of effort.

Search has become the key to unlocking the vast chest of information online.

For the searcher to find the information, it has to pop up. That's when the term *metadata* comes in to play. Metadata are key words that are used to label data, and right now it works quite well for text. Every Web page has key words linked to it that the creator of the page has assigned. However, it is still difficult to find audio/video, video, audio and other non-text information, as the ability to add key words is still undeveloped but now evolving in those content areas.

You know that tagging has become important when Ellen DeGeneres is talking about it on her show *Ellen*. She was explaining to her audience that once you tag a video, all someone has to do is search for that tag name using a video search engine. Actually, it was less an explanation and more a complaint, because if it's a picture that you really do *not* want the whole world to see, too bad. The whole world *can* see it once it is online and tagged.

## Data Exhaust

All those clicks that you make on the Internet are not lost on search engines like Google, Yahoo!, AOL, and Microsoft's Bing.

Those clicks are known as data exhaust, and they are gold to companies. It can be gold to you, if you take some time.

Where is data exhaust?

Do you want to find out popular sites on Google? First, you will have to turn off the instant search function of Google to get these responses. Then type in one letter—A or B, for example—and the most popular searches that begin with A or B pop up. Here are the results from that search exercise in Washington, D.C.

**Data Detective with Google**

| Letter A | Letter B |
| --- | --- |
| Amazon | Bank of America |
| AOL | Best Buy |
| American Airlines | Bing |
| AKO | Bed Bath and Beyond |
| Apple | BB&T |
| ATT | Bolt Bus |
| American Express | Borders |
| ABC | Barnes and Noble |
| Air Tran | BBC |

## Alerts

Search engines offer a service called alerts. Alerts are content management systems. By choosing a subject such as India or China, you are automatically notified when new content is posted about this subject. This new content comes from a variety of sources, including news wires, television news, general Internet content, and blogs.

You can also subscribe to more general alerts. One such alert is called a news alert, which alerts you to breaking news. Each search engine has its own set of alert categories.

## Social Media

Social media can also be seen as a digital workhorse. You can connect with many people by effectively using these social media sites.

Each social networking site has its own strengths and its own focus. Current popular sites are MySpace, Facebook, LinkedIn, YouTube and Twitter.

## Synchronization Across Devices

The ability for the BlackBerry to synchronize the contacts file with a PC is one reason the device took off in popularity.

As more and more devices become available, especially inexpensive devices such as netbooks, the ability to synchronize information between two or more devices is critical.

Areas when synchronization is important include:

- Contact files

- Favorites files or bookmark files

- Folders

- Calendar features such as Outlook

- E-mail

Synchronization should be a slam dunk, requiring virtually no learning curve. After all, the easier it is to synchronize devices, the more devices will be sold. Sadly, the user-friendly aspect of synchronization is still evolving.

## Devices Communicating with One Another

Beyond synchronization is something called devices communicating with one another. Bill Gates thinks this will be very important in the future. Wouldn't it be nice if there were a key on your PC that you could push and information would be downloaded to your digital TV, your smart phone or both? Or, say, you make a change in your calendar on one device and it automatically sends that update to all appropriate devices.

Such device to device communication is one of those attractions that is coming soon, but not real soon.

## Customized Home Pages

You can customize a home page such as My Yahoo! with lots of information. By adding news feeds (see instructions on the Web site on how to do this), you can track the highlights of your favorite industry online magazine or other type of online journal.

You can also keep informed about the companies that you are invested in or might wish to invest in or are simply interested in following.

In addition, online calendars and many other features are available.

## "Web Employment"

Hiring virtual assistants can make your life easier. This workhorse is also known as outsourcing your life. Timothy Ferriss, entrepreneur and author of *The 4-Hour Workweek,* says smart use of virtual assistants is key to efficiency in the digital age. From the title of his book, you already know his philosophy: you can greatly cut down the hours that you work in a week and still be very productive. Granted, the book is geared toward those who have their own companies, but the ideas can work for others as well.

As an aside, I do not really believe that you can have a four-hour work week on a consistent basis, no matter how many virtual assistants you have. I do think that overworking is unproductive in the digital age and that having "downtime" to reflect, digest, and allow your unconscious mind to work for you is critical.

## Data Hubs

A data hub is a site that you find on the Internet that allows you access to a large amount of information.

Check out your local library's Web site. It has likely gone through some dramatic changes, as more and more information comes online.

Google Books and Amazon have big goals for more and more books online. That's just books. Museums and other large institutions are putting their information online as well. Just explore, for example, the site: HermitageMuseum.org.

Why not just have one Web site that links to all the online knowledge in the world and in multiple languages?

That project—the World Digital Library (wdl.org)—is already under way. And, even if this project isn't successful because it has come slightly too soon and may be taking on too massive a task, there will be dozens of others like it.

The mission of the World Digital Library is to take all the primary resources of humankind such as documents, photographs, maps, musical scores, films, recordings, books and make them available online. According to futurist Paul Saffo, it is being touted as an "intellectual cathedral." The six official languages for the site are English, French, Spanish, Chinese, Russian and Arabic.

Data hubs such as the World Digital Library are great digital workhorses. Look for data hubs on the Internet. Finding them will help you make the most of your time—and they may turn you into a digital detective!

## Becoming a Digital Detective

The key is to find trends or anomalies in massive amounts of data. That's the kind of analysis that is powerful. That's what insurance companies do. They know how expensive your car is and how that information links to whether you might file a false accident report. They know when—that is, what day of the week—people tend to file false reports. This information all comes from analyzing data.

That's the goal here—find the kind of information that is powerful and then leverage it.

---

To leverage knowledge with the digital
mindset, become a digital detective.

Source: ingleyCONSULTANCY

---

## Making the Shift to Employing Digital Workhorses

Employing digital workhorses is important today and will become even more important as information online proliferates.

Here are some questions to ask yourself.

1. Do I currently employ digital workhorses?

    *My answer:* I employ as many as I can but have found that there is a point of diminishing returns. You can only keep up in a certain number of subject areas. Despite that, using a lot of alerts doesn't have to be distracting. They can always be saved and read later. I have not yet hired a virtual assistant, but I have hired contractors from online information that I found about them.

2. What do I see as the long-term benefit of digital workhorses?

*My answer:* I see more and more different types of digital workhorses becoming available to us. Some of these workhorses in the future will proactively "guess" what you and I want next. I see the benefit as changing lives for the better—and making things easier all the way around.

# Track the Trends

Tracking the trends is the next step for retooling and rewiring for the digital mindset.

Its importance lies in the sheer mass of information "out there." Even if you have gone through the steps of leveraging infinity by creating a big picture, putting together a list of questions and seeking answers online, you still may have more questions than answers. Or you might not really know what it all means.

The information that you are collecting must be seen in the context of current and future trends.

It is from knowing these trends that you will be able to discern if what you are doing is on the right track.

If you are looking at the big picture of getting a new job, then knowing the trends about the job area in which you are seeking, the trends of the current economy, the trends of the future economy, and the trends of the global economy are all critical to succeeding in your goal of getting a job.

But with information so accessible and the world moving so quickly, are there even any trends anymore? That's where the concepts of the un-trend and now trending come in.

## The Un-Trend and Now Trending

The un-trend is actually why you have to track trends in the first place. Because of the easy accessibility of digital information, it is more difficult to understand, quantify, or qualify the likes, dislikes, and tastes of the more than 310 million Americans who pride themselves on being individualists. This is not even mentioning the rest of the world which is also dealing with these same issues. Finding trends in an un-trend environment isn't easy, but it is possible.

Then, there is now the concept of "now trending." Web portals such as Yahoo! let you know what is currently a popular search. These are "mini" daily trends. Perhaps there is nothing truly profound in these mini-trends, but if you notice something unusual about them, then you may have stumbled on some important information.

There is a way to look for this "something unusual."

## Something Unusual

A one-minute video, created by Christopher Chabris and Daniel Simons, both cognitive psychologists, shows two teams passing basketballs. One team is dressed in black shirts, and the other team is dressed in white shirts. In the middle of the video, a female dressed in a full-body gorilla suit walks across the playing area. She stops in the middle, thumps her chest, and then walks away. The entire time that she appears in the video is about nine seconds. This is definitely something unusual in the midst of a video. This one-minute video was replicated and viewed by students around the Harvard University campus. After having chosen either the black shirt team or the white shirt team, they were asked to watch the video and count how many passes occurred in one minute. What amazed the creators of the video is that about 50% of the student viewers did not see the gorilla. Chabris and Simons have gone on to write a book entitled *The Invisible Gorilla*, expanding on this idea.

If you are *not* looking for something in a sea of data, you may not find it, although it may well be sitting there right in front of you, thumping its chest so to speak. The key is to be creative and ask unusual questions. Without unusual questions, you will miss the unusual.

If you are in the diamond business, you know that you have to sift through a lot of dirt to find the prize. That's exactly the same process to use when you look at masses of information.

The key is to sift through mountains of data, have a plan, know you can find something unusual, and you will.

Something you hope not to miss, but that is actually quite hard to see or predict, is the "sweet spot" of the hockey stick, also known as the tipping point.

## The Hockey Stick

The tipping point idea, made well known by Malcolm Gladwell, has been around a long time in the business world. It has traditionally been referred to as the hockey stick.

If you are looking for a really big opportunity, you will want to follow a trend at its "sweet spot," or the point of dramatic change.

The crook or the elbow of a hockey stick is its sweet spot. Here is a picture of it.

## Hockey Stick and Sweet Spot

"sweet spot"

Source: ingleyCONSULTANCY

If you are able to leverage trends at the sweet spot of the hockey stick—or at the beginning point of dramatic growth—then, with the appropriate strategy, you will have an opportunity for big success.

---

Leverage trends at the "sweet spot" of the hockey stick for an opportunity for big success.

Source: ingelyCONSULTANCY

---

Finding these sweet spots is not easy. It takes a willingness to look at masses of information. Acting on a sweet spot before the growth happens is an act of faith. You may get it right or you may not.

Even if you are not so concerned about the sweet spot, trends are critical for knowing what kind of questions to ask given a big-picture problem or issue you have targeted.

How does one start?

## A Trend Files or Folders

A good way to start the process of evaluating trends is to create a trend folder with subfolders for each trend area. Your folders can be electronic, physical or both.

If you are a nurse, your folders or files may be put together as follows:

Folder:      Trends

Subfolder:   Trends in the Nursing Industry in
             the United States

Subfolder:   Global Nursing Industry Trends

Subfolder:     Health Insurance Trends

Subfolder:     Health Care Trends

Subfolder:     Medication Trends

Subfolder:     Pain Management Trends

Subfolder:     Hospital Trends

Of course, this list is just a beginning.

Everyone who takes on the digital mindset needs to get their arms around the current and future trends of the digital toolbox.

The following sections discuss some digital trends as well as more general trends of the general population. The caveat here is that this is my view of the world. Your point of view, which may be entirely different, is the most critical.

## Digital TV Trends

This might sound confusing, but it is likely that mainstream TV may stay broadcast versus integrated into the Internet. It could be that there will be, down the line, what is known as classic over-the-air digital TV (such as NBC, CBS, ABC, and Fox), classic cable TV and classic satellite TV. The concept of "TV anywhere," however, will use the Internet, and more and more TV will be available on the Web, on your smart phone as well as on other devices.

Still, digital TVs do and will continue to have broadband Internet capabilities, but that is, again, likely to stay separate. With Sony Internet TV (digital TV with broadband Internet capabilities), you will be able to surf the Web in a "picture-in-picture" format—not a true integration. There are some that think that traditional TV may be going away, but that almost certainly will not happen. Digital TV will continue to evolve as "TV anywhere," but there will likely still be the traditional form of television. The pricing model, however, may evolve slightly differently in the future. For example, if you have a cable TV subscription, the subscription would enable you to view cable TV programs on diverse devices.

## Internet Trends

It is forecasted that there will be more and more search requests for video clips, audio clips, and images. There will also be more search requests from other areas. For example, Google is working on a project called Google Visual Search whereby you can use your smart phone camera to take a picture. Google recognizes the image and then sends you information about the image. In principle, Visual Search works if you are taking a picture of the Santa Monica pier or even if you are taking a picture of a book. The service is still under development.

Another area of the Internet that is changing quickly is the so-called cloud. An example of the cloud is Internet storage such as Google Docs or Box.net. Storing information in the cloud will mean that one is linked less to a particular device and more to devices in the plural, with the ability to access information much more easily than today.

## PC Trends

The idea of a PC will broaden, according to Bill Gates and it will take advantage of nearby display and projection surfaces. One such device is called Microsoft Surface. Gates describes Microsoft Surface as a, "table-shaped computer on which you use gestures, touch and objects to manipulate information." The Surface allows multiple users to interact with each other and with digital content in a simple way.

Another area in which the PC has shifted is the program that MIT Media Lab founder Nicolas Negroponte established entitled One Laptop for Every Child. Recently, he has shifted his thinking to a tablet such as the iPad for every child.

## Broadband Internet Service Trends

Coming in the near future of broadband is a concept called universal broadband—or broadband for everybody.

Universal broadband is controversial because the Federal Communications Commission is proposing that universal service subsidies for phone service be used to fund broadband instead. It is partly controversial because many Americans do not know about universal service subsidies for phone service.

The shift in thinking is that heretofore everyone in the United States was believed to have the right to phone service. Now the thinking is that everyone has the right to broadband Internet service.

65% of Americans currently have broadband Internet at home.

## Creativity, Flexibility, and Being Good with People Trend

As more and more companies take on the digital mindset, they will be looking for those qualities that can survive in the sea of infinity. Those qualities are creativity, flexibility and being good with people.

Creativity is necessary because it is one way in which to make sense of the current information by mixing and matching it in new ways.

Flexibility is important because sometimes a product or service is released that changes one's thinking. You have to be flexible enough to take on this new mode of thinking quite quickly. In fact, taking on a new product or service works best by assimilating it at the moment when you learn about it.

Finally, being good with people is going to be even more important in the future than it is today. People skills will become more valuable, not less, partly because, via e-mail, social media, and the Internet, one is in contact with so many others.

## Getting Boys' Attention Trend

A recent trend is that fewer young males are going to first-run movies. But it isn't just the movie industry that avidly tracks what young males do. According to *BusinessWeek*, "boys (or their parental proxies) are ravenous consumers who spend billions each year on apparel, toys, and video games."

It is estimated that there are about 30 million young males (aged 5 to 19) in the United States.

## Children Getting Older at a Younger Age/ Adults Staying Younger at an Older Age Trend

Only a little more than a hundred years ago, much was expected from children. They were seen as little adults and were expected to work and live as adults did. Today's concept is completely different. Childhood is considered a time of innocence, and that innocence is nurtured. Childhood is also all about play and imagination. It is a time of protection by adults.

In the digital arena, however, children are now getting older at a younger age and adults are staying younger at an older age. Technology is the great equalizer.

If you understand this digital mindset trend—children getting older at a younger age and adults staying younger at an older age—then you may see that there are many implications of this trend. For example, there may be growth in the electronic toy industry for adults over the next ten years.

Speaking of toys, another toy trend is "going upstream," when, rather than a movie or TV show generating toys, the opposite happens. Toys generate movies and TV shows.

## The Next Industrial Revolution Trend

Although the information revolution has been on the rise in the United States, the country's industrial side has been in decline. Yet it is possible that there will be a new industrial revolution, albeit a much different one than the first. It is possible that once ideas and prototypes are tested, small companies, such as those developed in a garages and basements, will turn overseas for production.

## The New Urbanism Trend

People are moving back to the cities, not just in the United States, but globally. Today, roughly half the world's population lives in urban areas, but by 2050, the United Nations predicts that two-thirds of the world's projected 9.2 billion people will reside in cities.

People who stay in small towns or remain in the suburbs of larger cities may find that their communities begin to have urban advantages. Urban planner Andres Duany has looked at what does and does not work in the suburbs. He sees the importance of making communities walkable. He believes that in the twenty-first century, "every residential unit will be a live-work unit."

## A Shortcut of Sorts

Knowing the trends is a way to cut through large amounts of data and figure out what it means. It is a shortcut of sorts.

If you know the trends, you have a better shot at finding a job niche with real growth opportunity. Tracking trends might help you in your current job. It might mean alerting others where you work to opportunities for growth that they might not be seeing. It might mean a promotion. Tracking trends might lead you to a great vacation. The process has unpredictable results, but it is a powerful filter of information.

The trends that have been presented and discussed here are just sample trends. The purpose is to get you thinking along these lines.

Knowing and tracking trends can be a proactive process, whereby you actively track trends. Or, when you derive trends from examining the data that you have collected, it can be more reactive. In your search, you are looking for the invisible gorilla.

There is a nugget of gold waiting for you. If you are looking at what you've been "told" to look for, as the Harvard University students were told to count the passes in the video, you may miss something critical.

## Making the Shift
## to Tracking the Trends

Tracking the trends is a challenging undertaking. It requires sorting through mountains of information and asking something unusual about that information.

Here are some questions to ask yourself.

1. Do I currently track trends?

*My answer:* I have been tracking trends for many years. Even when it doesn't directly apply to what I am doing at the time, I have continued to track trends. By knowing the trends, it is easier to sift through a lot of information quickly and see what I am interested in. Tracking trends allows me to write my business plans more accurately. This system plays an integral part in the books I write.

2. Do I have a system for tracking trends?

*My answer:* I use both computer files and physical files to keep track of trends. I also spend time rearranging files to see if I can find unusual links or see some sort of connection that could be easily missed.

# Mesh the Digital Mindset with Mobility

Mobile devices allowing you to receive and transmit digital audio/video, digital data, and digital voice anywhere in the United States and the world have profound implications on all aspects of your life. That and the sheer number of mobile devices make knowing how to leverage mobility exceedingly important.

## Mobile versus Wireless

At first blush, the two words—*mobile* and *wireless*—seem the same. After all, some folks call their cell phones wireless phones, some call them mobile phones, and some might simply say "my mobile." It seems these words are interchangeable.

However, mobile and wireless are *not* interchangeable words. Desktop PCs can be connected wirelessly to a broadband Internet service, but they are not mobile. Satellite dishes receiving a satellite TV signal in your backyard are wireless devices, and they are certainly not mobile.

Mobility refers here to wireless devices that are small enough to make them easily carried.

The major reason mobility appears on the radar screen of the digital mindset is that some of the major devices of the digital age—smart phones, tablets, and laptop PCs—are mobile.

And one of these mobile devices—the smart phone—has just gone through a true revolution in sheer market size.

## A Revolution within a Revolution

Actually, two revolutions are happening at the same time. The larger one, of course, is the digital revolution that is the focus of this book. But another revolution brews within the digital revolution and is fueled by digits. This is the mobile revolution.

To get a handle on any revolution, you have to have an endgame in sight. The one for the mobile revolution can be seen as both a short-term endgame and long-term endgame.

The short-term endgame is: Every person in the world will own and use a mobile device. These mobile devices will have the triple play of: digital TV, broadband Internet, and voice services. Why short term?

Look where we are already. Globally, there are 4.6 billion mobile devices in a world population for 2011 estimated to be 7 billion. Currently, many of these 4.6 billion mobile phones are not smart phones. But the world is moving to having all phones be smart— smart in the sense of being able to send and receive the triple play. Keep in mind that many people have more than one mobile phone, so the penetration isn't quite as high as it seems. But don't let this fool you. The mobile phone world moves with lightening speed.

The long-term endgame for smart phones is anyone's guess. What will the world be like when everyone is connected to vast amounts of digital information that can be mixed and matched in an infinite number of ways? Will peace reign in the world? Will everyone get along better? Will everyone *not* get along better? Which countries will go through the biggest changes?

To really appreciate this revolution and to see how far the world has come in a very short time, look to some history. Mobile phone service evolved from the landline phone business, and that's where the story begins.

## Setting the Mobile Phone Stage

Before AT&T's divestiture in 1983 when competition entered the phone business, AT&T was a monopoly phone company in the United States. For most of this time, that role worked and AT&T did a superb job. With Bell Labs as a research and development arm, AT&T had creative and innovative characteristics and was a steady, reliable company.

In 1947, Bell Labs came up with the idea of expanding the landline phone business of AT&T to include a cellular phone business. Their idea was to divide U.S. geography into smaller areas or cells. Each of these areas would have its own base station or cell tower. There was a small glitch, however. What happens when you are in the middle of a cell phone call and move from one cell to another? There was no technology in 1947 that would allow this hand-off from cell to cell.

Nonetheless, AT&T gave the Bell Labs proposal for this cellular system to the Federal Communications Commission for approval and permission to move forward. But in an almost frightening example of bureaucratic red tape, the Federal Communications Commission did not take action for 21 years.

Meanwhile, other parts of the world, Sweden in particular and Scandinavia in general, took note of the Bell Labs ideas. By 1956, Sweden had two commercial cellular systems in test operation. Cell phones were installed in cars, and the radius was one cell, eliminating the need to transfer calls from one cell to another. Even though this system, limited as it was, stayed in use for more than a decade, there were only 125 subscribers at the end of the trial. The Swedish trials were a harbinger of things to come, however, as what ultimately came from these early experiments was a global wireless standard—GSM—that virtually all countries in the 1990s adopted, except the United States.

Eventually, the Federal Communications Commission did act. Yes, the agency moved slowly in the beginning (and the consequences of those early decisions are still with us) but the pace did pick up—considerably. Although there was excitement about the technology, no one really predicted a revolution. Early on, a consulting study done for AT&T forecast one million cellular phone subscribers by the year 2000.

## Size of the Smart Phone Market

By 1985, there were 340,213 cell phone subscribers in the United States. As of June 2010, there were 292.8 million subscribers to a device that is less cell phone and more smart phone. If this doesn't sound dramatic, check out the chart on page 142.

This is just looking at the hardware for wireless service. What has happened only since 2005 in the United States is a dramatic growth in wireless data services. On smart phones, there is now more *wireless data* traffic transmitted and received than *voice* traffic.

Currently, there are two major components of wireless data: text and e-mail. In 2005, text messages totaled 57 million. That has grown dramatically to 1,806 billion (or 1.806 trillion) text messages in the 12 months ending in June 2010. There are almost as many text messages sent as minutes spent talking on smart phones.

If you bundle messaging (text and e-mail) with all the other data transmitted, the total amount of wireless data transmitted in the first six months of 2010 was 161.2 billion megabytes. According to Robert Roche, Vice President, Research at *CTIA—The*

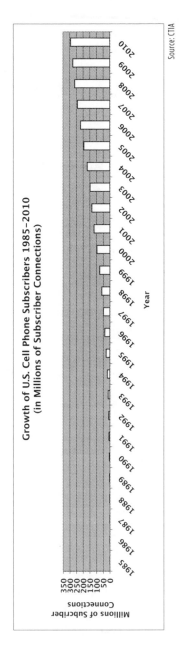

Growth of U.S. Cell Phone Subscribers 1985–2010
(in Millions of Subscriber Connections)

Source: CTIA

*Wireless Association©,* "If one megabyte is seen as a 4-inch candy bar and you stood them on top of one another, these 161.2 billion megabytes would reach from the earth to the moon and back. . . . not once but twenty-one times."

As startlingly as this growth is, it doesn't compare with what has been happening in many countries of the world. The United States has only about one-third the mobile phone subscribers as China does and about one-half as India does. In total, there are 4.6 billion mobile phones globally. Doesn't it make sense to pay attention to such a phenomenon?

## More Types of Mobile Devices

The major categories of mobile devices include mobile/smart phones, PCs (Windows and Macs), and tablets. More and more types of mobile devices are coming quickly to the marketplace. E-books are an example of a growing category.

Other portable devices important in the market may or may not have wireless Internet connections. Examples of such portable devices include MP3 players, handheld game consoles, portable DVD players, handheld GPS devices, and a host of other portables.

## Shift in Players

Scandinavia got a head start early on in the mobile arena, and until recently, that part of Europe has led the mobile market globally. Nokia, a Finnish corporation, is still the 800-pound gorilla in the middle of the room. Right now, there are 1.3 billion Nokia mobile phones worldwide.

But the United State may not be left out of a leadership role much longer. Silicon Valley is roaring back. The iPhone from Apple powered by software known as iOS (the OS stands for operating system) has been phenomenally successful, but now there's a new smart phone. This new smart phone is overtaking the iPhone and it's powered by the Android mobile phone platform, which comes from Google. The business plan developed by Google is to give away the platform to its hardware partners. Google will make money from Android in other ways, primarily from the Internet, and more specifically from search engine ad revenues. This give-away of Android software may work and Google needs to be watched carefully. Microsoft is also behind the scenes with its own software, currently Windows Phone 7.

As you likely have discerned, the competitive environment for the mobile phone is cut-throat, fast changing, and unforgiving of missteps.

## Becoming Distance Insensitive

As mobile devices make everyone more and more distance insensitive, corporate America struggles with the implications. Entrepreneur Timothy Ferriss, author of *The 4-Hour Work Week*, understands this struggle. The book's major thesis is that life gets richer if you take advantage of the mobility provided by today's technology and if you stop wasting your time. He is convinced there is a lot of "busyness" going on in U.S. companies, and he is likely right. Much of the corporate world has yet to acknowledge the power of downtime even while you're on the job.

Strangely, mobility and addressing busyness are tied together. Although it certainly depends on your profession and career, a great deal of work can be accomplished with just a broadband-capable PC and a smart phone. Being able to carry a PC and smart phone with you is transforming the business world. It is also transforming people's lives as they strive to find a work/home balance by geographically leveraging the utility of these devices. Strategizing with your boss and colleagues about how to make use of the power of mobility is key, but this conversation is less likely to occur if everyone is caught up in mundane and unimportant tasks. Sadly, the work world can get too busy to see applications of the positive aspects of mobility.

## Growth in Services

Recent growth in mobile services is related to Internet access, audio/video, and apps. More and more mobile phones have Internet access. As for audio/video, mobile TV is still in its infancy. Apps, driven initially by the iPhone, have grown exponentially. The iPhone in 2010 had more than 300,000 apps. Interestingly, the Google Android phone had far fewer, in 2010 only 70,000 apps. At issue here may be the digital mindset toolbox. Google does not have the background in hardware that Apple does, but watch carefully. In late 2010, Android-platform mobile phones began overtaking the iPhone in monthly sales, so the apps ratio between the iPhone and Android is likely to change quickly.

## Your Own Mobility

How are you going to leverage mobile devices so they serve you rather than you serving them? No one wants to be a slave to a device or feel tethered to a communications network.

Determining when you answer your smart phone, when you respond to e-mails, when you write and send e-mails or text messages, and when you check for voice mails and e-mails/text messages has a profound impact on your life. A custom design for handling your mobility can be created. It is a custom design oriented toward what serves you best. Creating voice messages and "out-of-office" e-mail responses that indicate when you will be checking or reading your messages and when you will be getting back to colleagues and friends is one way to manage the onslaught of communication in the digital age. Find a way to have your mobility serve you. Leveraging social media is another way to have mobility serve you. Look for a dramatic shift in use of social media as it becomes more and more accessible via smart phones.

One issue is clear: You can get very busy with these tools, but you also run the risk of getting too busy and not accomplishing much. As soon as you move away from the big-picture aspects of your life, you may end up wasting time. Focus on the big picture and manage your mobile connections such that you keep interruptions to a minimum.

## Lifestyle Changes

As the smart phone gets smarter, as PCs get smaller, and as more devices that are currently portable become mobile as well, you become, in some ways, untethered. A recent consulting project took me to New Hampshire for two and a half months. The ease in which I could be away from my home and office was astonishing. Smart phones and broadband-capable laptop PCs facilitate being away. Note: for long periods, bring loved ones and/or pets if you can—it makes a huge difference.

But what's the real future of mobility?

## Future of Mobility in a Nutshell

Part of the future of mobility lies in the software or operating system that runs a smart phone. Apple's iOS, Microsoft's Windows Phone 7, and Google's Android are in a fierce battle behind the scenes. They are battling for your mobility dollar.

The real future of mobility goes hand in hand with software. The capabilities of smart phones via the development of the operating systems will become more and more sophisticated. The future will be less and less about the triple play and more and more about the connection of a mobile device to hundreds of other devices. In the not too distant future, much of what goes on with your handset may not be noticed immediately by you. Your mobile device will be busy connecting and talking with other devices, dutifully completing tasks you previously have assigned.

The mobile device just may end up being one of the biggest and best digital workhorses of all.

## Making the Shift to Meshing the Digital Mindset with Mobility

You may be feeling somewhat dizzy about all the changes going on in the mobile environment. I know I do. Here are some questions to ask yourself.

1. Do my mobile devices serve me or do I serve them?

   *My answer*: I confess that the BlackBerry changed my life. Before the BlackBerry, I spent more time than I wanted checking my e-mail. Now, when I check my e-mails, it takes me less than 30 seconds. Although the addictive aspect of a Blackberry has earned it the nickname CrackBerry, I call it my SlackBerry. It saves me so much time, energy, and effort—I almost feel like a slacker.

2. How do I currently leverage mobility?

   *My answer:* I leverage mobility by having times when I am completely online and very accessible as opposed to times when I am offline and not accessible. This means I do not always have my smart phone with me. This works for me because I am usually prompt responding to people once I am back online.

# Live the Digital Mindset Life

Home is where the heart is. So it is with the digital mindset. It travels with you wherever you go.

How it affects virtually everything has been the subject of this book.

For the digital mindset life to work over the long haul, however, it must meet certain basic emotional needs.

## Meeting Basic Emotional Needs

Over the long term, the digital mindset life must meet the two basic emotional needs of humans: heroism and connection. The importance of these two basic emotional needs appears to be reversed according to gender. Men tend to value heroism first and then connection.

Women tend to value connection first and then heroism. Whatever the order, they are very important to both genders.

Taking on the digital mindset can be seen as a small act of heroism. It requires changing one's perspective about everything, no easy feat. It is a quiet, personal victory, but a victory nonetheless. It creates a framework for future victories and future acts of heroism.

Granted, it is traditional to think of a hero as someone who saves a life from a fire or wins a battle in a war. But heroism means so much more in modern life. It might mean winning a business contract, bringing home the bacon, or raising a child successfully. What will the new heroism be in the context of the digital mindset? It must evolve in some way to meet this most basic of needs.

Connection occurs easily with the digital mindset. All the different devices and systems make it easy to communicate. Yet the deeper, more intimate connection that everyone craves occurs outside the context of actively using digital assets. This aspect of life must be cherished and nurtured as it can easily get lost in the demands of the digital mindset lifestyle.

Will I be a happy camper if my most basic emotional needs are met along with having the keys to the kingdom of infinite possibilities? As Sarah Palin would say: you betcha!

## Recap

So far, the digital mindset has taken you through nine steps. These steps have been:

1. Embrace infinity.

2. Leverage infinity.

3. Rewire your brain for the digital mindset.

4. Take on the digital mindset toolbox.

5. Make organization a top priority.

6. Layer creativity into your life.

7. Employ digital workhorses.

8. Track the trends.

9. Mesh the digital mindset with mobility.

Thomas Edison once said, "Opportunity is missed by most people because it is dressed in overalls and looks like work." The digital mindset *is* dressed in overalls and it *is* work. But the work that you do to acquire the digital mindset will pay off in many, many ways.

The digital mindset means taking on all of these nine steps and living your life that way. Once you do this, you will begin to notice an excitement, a sense of control, and a feeling of a real new beginning.

Even if you choose to be disconnected for a time, you still can carry with you the digital mindset. In fact, being disconnected from time to time may be part of a strategy that you put together for yourself. This could be a certain time daily, on the weekends or whatever suits your schedule.

There is some more good news about the digital mindset. Oliver Wendell Holmes said, "We do not quit playing because we get old. We get old because we quit playing."

The digital mindset is about being *in the game* and you may just notice that you are looking younger, even if you are still quite young, or, for that matter, quite old.

The digital mindset also introduces some bigger issues such as trust.

Trust has become a large issue in the digital age, simply because there are so many scams, spam, phishing, and who know what else may come down the pike.

It would be easy to say: Just keep track of them all. But that's not possible.

The one anchor that you have is yourself. In the sea of infinity, staying true to yourself is your anchor. The digital mindset works best if you never compromise yourself. There is a big difference between compromising and compromising yourself. Staying true to yourself is another way of saying: I never compromise myself.

But how do you actually use this digital mindset?

Let's start with a concrete example of how the digital mindset can be used.

## The Digital Mindset and the Automobile Industry

The grand tumble of the automobile industry in 2008 is one example of the digital mindset *not* at work. What happened to General Motors and the other U.S. car companies? Many would say that they didn't listen to U.S. consumers. Many would say they were stodgy in the way they ran their companies. There has been a whole litany of reasons discussed in the media.

Now put on the digital mindset. Now, as you are thinking about the digital mindset that is supported by digital assets, it will become obvious that there are a few more things on the minds of Americans than a big home and a nice car.

Many digital assets are not inexpensive. Hence, the home dollar is not just going to food, clothing, shelter (a house or an apartment, in general), transportation (traditionally, a car) and a few other necessities. It is also going to digital assets: hardware, software, services, content, and accessories. Again, these are not inexpensive items.

So, what the auto industry has not kept up with is disposable dollars that Americans have. There are fewer dollars for transportation. More specifically, there are fewer dollars for new cars.

Granted, this is just one perspective of a complex issue. Still, the auto industry may have to proactively figure out the American consumer's wallet in the digital age. Of note is that Japanese car companies are having trouble luring their own twenty-something generation into buying cars. You can guess what the young Japanese are buying instead!

## Old Think Versus New Think

Once you take the digital mindset on, you begin to see—drum roll, please—not. . . . everyone. . . . has.

In fact, when you encounter someone caught up in "old think," it may be like hearing a note badly out of tune. It will sound so "off" that it will make you cringe.

Current examples are everywhere. Right now, when I hear the phrase, "Main Street and Wall Street are on disconnect," I cringe. That's not the issue, I think to myself. The issue is that neither Main Street nor Wall Street has embraced the digital mindset. Both "streets" are on disconnect with what's happening around them before they even try to connect with one another.

Almost all financial gurus of our time do not talk about the digital mindset nor do they talk about the importance of your digital assets. Americans are influenced by these financial gurus and it is important for them to take on this new mindset.

Who else are Americans influenced by? Certainly politicians and celebrities play a large role.

President Barack Obama, Vice President Joe Biden, Secretary of State Hillary Clinton, the governors of the 50 states, Senator John McCain, former Governor Sarah Palin, and Nancy Pelosi are just a very few of the influential politicians of our time.

Who are the biggest celebrities now? The list is long. It includes Brad Pitt, George Clooney, Angelina Jolie, Jennifer Aniston, Megan Fox, Jessica Simpson, Tom Cruise, Tom Hanks as some well known actors. Who are big money making singers? Madonna, Lady Gaga, Jennifer Lopez, Barbra Streisand, Justin Timberlake, Beyonce, Taylor Swift, Tim McGraw, and Kenny Chesney are some. Who are important newscasters? Diane Sawyer, Katie Couric, Matt Lauer, and

Meredith Viera come to mind. Who are big directors? James Cameron, Steven Spielberg, and George Lucas are a few. Who are important TV personalities? Ellen de Generes, Oprah, Dr. Phil, Rachel Ray, and Dr. Drew are widely known.

Who, out of this list, are *new think* as in the digital mindset or *old think* as in brick-and-mortar thinking? And why is this important? It is important because so many people watch and listen to well-known personalities.

Not to put these folks on the spot, but they are, in fact, on the spot.

Yet no one is as important as you. You are in the control seat of your life and you can do this or not.

Perhaps you are doing most of this already. Kudos to you, then. If not, now is the time.

## Reaching a Critical Mass or "Tipping Point"

Many are frustrated right now about the economy and about the job market.

Nothing will happen of significance with the U.S. job market and its economy until the tipping point is reached for the digital mindset. Enough of the populace must take this on for the recovery to really take off.

---

The number of citizens in the United States who have taken on the digital mindset must reach the tipping point before the economy and job market will recover.

Source: ingleyCONSULTANCY

---

Once this tipping point is reached, the game will have changed. People will have stopped asking, "Where is my job?" and started asking, "What kind of job can I create for myself?"

## No One Left Behind

Former President George W. Bush created the program No Child Left Behind. For the digital mindset, no one should be left behind.

It cannot be forgotten that the majority of the world's population are hungry, illiterate and poor.

The United States owes it to the world to lead in this area. There must be a way to stimulate our own economy *and* help the hungry, illiterate, and poor within and outside of our borders. It takes a plan.

## Infinite Possibilities

Novelist and essayist C.S. Lewis said that you are never too old to set another goal or to dream a new dream.

If you take on the digital mindset, the world is at your finger tips. The digital mindset allows you to more easily set another goal or dream another dream.

Beyond goals and dreams, something about the digital mindset gives a person a zest for life. You feel more stylish, smarter. This new mindset makes you more daring, more curious and more cutting edge.

You may crave the best that life has to offer—and desire to give that best to all. The digital mindset can allow that to happen.

You are a fisherman in the sea of knowledge with the digital mindset. Or, you can stay on the shore telling fish stories.

Your choice. Either you are in the game of life—and that game now means you take on the digital mindset—or you stay on the sidelines.

The digital mindset is the great equalizer of our age. You may be eighteen. You may be eighty. You may have a lot of money. You may not

With the digital mindset, it doesn't matter.

It is all about infinite possibilities. . . .

# Index

printers, 63
proactive, 3, 120, 132, 153
project management, 86

# R

radio, 8, 9, 10, 27, 34, 67–
    69, 70
radio programs, 8, 68, 770
Ray, Rachel, 155
Reactive, 3, 132
*Reinventing the Body,*
    *Resurrecting the Soul,* 54
retreat, 19, 21, 22
rewire, 41–62, 151
rewiring, 1, 41, 42, 51, 54,
    59, 121
right-brained, 42, 43, 49, 50
right-handed, 43, 60
Roche, Robert, 139

# S

Sacks, Oliver, 58
Saffo, Paul, 118
salary, 26
satellite TV, zi, 9, 27, 66,
    126, 136
Sawyer, Diane, 154
school information, 82
*Scientific American,* 45, 58, 59
search engines, 110–114
services, xi, 6, 14, 26, 61–63,
    66–68, 73, 74, 76, 83,
    84, 96, 101, 136, 139,
    143, 153
shortcuts, 3
shortcutting , 3
Simons, Daniel, 123
simplicity, 17
Simpson, Jessica, 154
SlackBerry, 146

smart phone, 9, 15, 16, 62,
    63, 65–67, 69, 74, 116,
    126, 127, 136, 137, 139,
    141–145, 147
Snider, Ray S., 45
social media, 37, 68, 110, 115,
    129, 144
software, 2, 15, 25, 26,
    61–63, 65, 66, 72–74, 76,
    82–84, 101, 102, 111, 142,
    145, 153
software developers, 25, 26
software development, 25
somersaults, 2
something unusual, 122–124,
    132
Sony PlayStation, 71
Spielberg, Steven, 155
spinning lady video, 42
status quo, ix, 32, 33
Stewart, Potter, 19
Streisand, Barbra, 154
structure, 43, 96, 100
Sweden, 138
sweet spot, 124, 125
Swift, Taylor, 154
synchronization across devices,
    110, 115

# T

tablets, 63, 64, 136, 141
telecommunications industry,
    xi, 7, 18, 21
terabyte, 110, 111
text, 2, 12, 62, 105, 110, 111,
    113, 139, 144
texting, 37
Timberlake, Justin, 154
time management, 86
tipping point, 10, 124, 155, 156
trend file, 125